DIVING
GOZO & COMINO

The essential guide to an underwater playground

Richard Salter

ISBN 978-1-909455-16-0 (Paperback)
ISBN 978-1-909455-17-7 (EPUB ebook)
ISBN 978-1-909455-18-4 (PDF ebook)

Cataloguing-In-Publication Data A catalogue record for this book can be obtained from the British Library.

Cover Design © 2017 Dived Up. Front cover: photo of Steve and Fiona Harris in Xlendi Tunnel by Rob Smith. Back: the author diving in the Karwela wreck by Jacek Madejski; scorpionfish by Catherine & Jean-Pierre Cornand.

Printed by Gutenberg, Malta.

Published 2017 by

Dived Up Publications
Oxford • United Kingdom
Email info@divedup.com
Web DivedUp.com

Contents

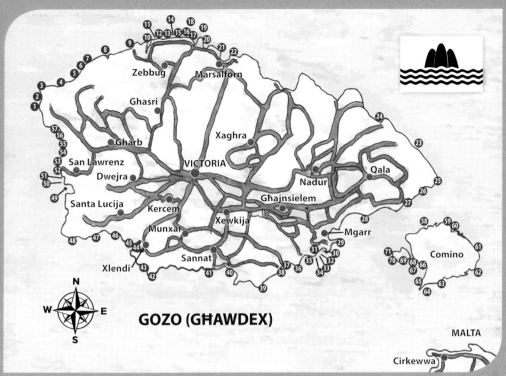

GOZO (GĦAWDEX)

MALTA

Cirkewwa

The Beautiful Island of Gozo

A pleasant ferry ride from Malta has brought travellers and underwater explorers seeking adventure and relaxation to Gozo for many years. Dramatic high cliffs, secluded bays and inlets, crystal clear waters, caves, caverns and rugged landscapes are a paradise for walkers, photographers, cyclists, climbers and especially for us divers who can explore the depths below.

During the spring the countryside erupts in a riot of colours. In summer the hot sun warms the sea and dries out the land. Then there are occasional outbursts of dramatic weather from October onwards. The winter can be dived but conditions can be rather unpredictable for a holiday destination.

The island is steeped in myth, history and culture dating back centuries and I include some information about places you might visit and things you will see and do. The historical relationship between the UK and Malta has resulted in a strong British influence: English is spoken by almost everyone, beer is sold in pints and driving is on the left. The food is just amazing, the currency is the Euro and about 100,000 European divers visit every year.

Voted by many as some of the best diving in Europe, Gozo is just as dramatic beneath the surface as it is above it. There are plenty of underwater attractions with the chance to explore many caves, tunnels, wrecks, reefs and bays. Combine this with the profuse amount of marine life and you have an underwater photographer's paradise all within a few seconds of leaving the surface.

I am an instructor and guide on Gozo myself, but I arrived to find accurate information and publications rather lacking. So I drew some maps and learned a little of the history so that I could show my customers. Then they could choose where to go depending on the kind of diving they wished to pursue, their qualification and experience and the weather conditions. My diving knowledge and experience has increased over the years and this I am glad to be able to pass on to you.

In this book I have tried to assist you in every way possible by including as much information as I can about approximate times, distances, depths and bearings. I give recommendations and advice but ultimately the way you conduct a dive is your choice. This book does not take the place of a trained professional who is accustomed to the local waters and procedures in Gozo. A local guide, with their experience and knowledge can show you the best routes to take on a particular day. Be warned: conditions and circumstances can change dramatically and there are some dive centres that will not accommodate unaccompanied divers for these reasons.

Whether you are a new visitor or a repeat diver over many years, I hope this guide will help you plan dives that you may not have had previous knowledge of and therefore give you many more options to choose from.

With that in mind — be safe and enjoy your Gozo experience!

Richard Salter
February 2017
gozo-guide.com
Facebook @GozoShoreDiveGuide

Acknowledgements

Thank you to all the diving centres on Gozo for giving me the opportunity and encouragement to pursue my dreams and goals. My gratitude also goes to all the staff, friends and customers who I have encountered over many years, enabling me to gain the knowledge and experiences that have made it possible for me to bring you this book.

My thanks must also go to the many contributors of photographs. They include: Pete Bullen (oceanfoto.co.uk), Catherine & Jean-Pierre Cornand, Andreas & Chantel Chioccetti, Christian Di Costanzo, Roy Davidson, Cathryn James, Jacek Madejski (jacek.madejski@gmail.com), Claudine Martin Le Coq, Joachim Neudert, David Rawle, Rob Smith (www.robsmith.co.uk) and Dr Vera Wittenburg.

My special thanks go to Mark Busittil and his boat *Divemania*, Tony Lautier of Neptune Boat Diving Services, Dennis Wiltshire of Lelux Bed and Breakfast, Josette Farrugia of Hakari Gozo, Agnieszka Kostera-Kosterzewska staff instructor at St Andrews, Claudio Dino Geletovic (old salt and good friend), Don Carless, Joseph A. Vella Gaffiero and Mick Gillen.

The credit for the inspiration to write this book must go to my father
Cecil Francis Salter (1939-2013).

Introduction

The dive sites are split into five geographical areas. Each area starts with a map showing the location of the sites in that section.

Dive site names

Where a dive site has a name (rather than just being a place) it is generally given in English (followed by Gozitan in brackets). In some cases it is a straight translation, but not always. Some sites have several names and I have included as many as I can in order to make it easier for you to ask directions and therefore find your way.

Maps

The suggested routes are approximate. They are not strictly to scale, but are an attempt to include all of the interesting features and topography. There will always be reasons to detour but I suggest you stick to the routes given until you are familiar with a particular dive site. Many dives can be done multiple ways but heed the advice given to help orientate yourself and avoid getting into trouble.

Key

Boat dive / shore dive / can be either	BOAT	SHORE	BOAT or SHORE
Suggested routes			
Swim-throughs or overhead environments			
Entry / exit / combined entry and exit			
Boat anchor points			
Distance between two points	40m		
Parking	P		

Boat dives

These are not recommended for self-guided diving — you should check with local dive shops to see what they are planning.

Metric/Imperial

This book gives metric measurements for the maps and general descriptions of dive sites. It also gives an approximate imperial conversion for the overall depths (under 'Details') for each site. Additional, simple approximate conversions can be made using the following rules: 3m = 10ft; 10m = 33ft.

ROB SMITH

Bimble –To amble without real aim.

Halocline – A halocline exists in most caverns that are situated along the cliffs on Gozo. Haloclines are made when fresh water from the land filters through the rock and enters the sea. The less dense fresh water forms a layer over the salt water from the ocean. If a diver passes through and disturbs these two layers his or her vision is often distorted.

Knights – Knights of the Order of Saint John, or to give them their full name, Order of Knights of the Hospital of Saint John of Jerusalem.

Posidonia/Neptune grass – The sea grass which is a common feature of the Mediterranean *(see 'Posidonia Oceanica' on page 168)*.

Thermocline – A body of water separated by two distinct or drastic changes in temperature. A diver passing through this line will feel a distinct temperature change.

Introduction

CATHERINE & JEAN PIERRE CORNAND

This book encourages cautious and respectful diving, in relation to both others and the environment. To safely conduct a dive, participants must be properly trained, be able to rely on their own abilities, and have knowledge of conditions at their chosen site.

I provide information to help and encourage the safe conduct of any dive but accept no responsibility for anyone who disregards their training, any safety advice given or takes unnecessary risks. If you are unsure about conditions or any dive site, seek help from a local dive centre or your affiliated diving organisation.

Diving Information

Dive Centres

Ghajnsielem

Extra Divers Gozo
Grand Hotel, St. Anthony Street
Tel: +356 2156 3840 / +356 9944 8767
gozo@extradivers.info
www.extradivers.info

Marsalforn

Atlantis Diving Centre
Qolla Street
Tel: +356 2155 4685 / +356 7956 2888
diving@atlantisgozo.com
www.atlantisgozo.com

Bubbles Dive Centre
17 Triq Il-Forn. Tel: +356 2702 8299
info@diving-gozo.com
www.diving-gozo.com

Calypso Diving Centre
The Seafront, Marsalforn Bay
Tel: +356 2156 1757 / +356 7956 1757
info@calypsodivers.com
www.calypsodivers.com

Family Diving Gozo
Tel +356 9913 3422
info@familydivinggozo.pl
www.nurkowanienagozo.pl

Gozo Aquasports
Green Valley, Rabat Road
Tel: +356 2156 3037 / +356 7956 3037
dive@gozoaquasports.com
www.gozoaquasports.com

Nautic Team Gozo Ltd.
(CMAS / IAC & TEC ITC IDDA Training
Centre), Volcano Street
Tel: +356 2155 8507
nautic@go.net.mt / www.nauticteam.com

Scuba Kings Gozo
46a Marina Street
Tel: +356 2126 1221 / +356 7956 1221
gozodiveschool@hotmail.com
www.divemalta-gozo.com

Qala

Blue Waters Dive Cove
Kuncizzjoni Street
Tel: +356 2156 5626 / +356 7953 6874
info@divebluewaters.com
www.divebluewaters.com

Xewkija

Gozo Diving
Mġarr Road
Tel: +356 7900 9565 / +356 7900 9575
www.gozotechnicaldiving.com
www.gozodiving.com
audrey@gozodiving.com

Xlendi

Gaulos Dive Cove
Marziena Street
Tel: +356 2155 5708 / +356 7909 3169
mariobugeja.mb@gmail.com
www.gaulosdivecove.com

Moby Dives
Xlendi Bay
Tel: +356 2155 1616 / +356 2156 4429
mobydives@gozo.com
www.mobydivesgozo.com

St Andrew's Divers Cove
St. Simon Street
Tel: +356 2155 1301
standrew@gozodive.com
www.gozodive.com

Utina Diving College
Calleja Building, Rabat Road
Tel: +356 2155 0514 / +356 7955 0514
utina@gozomail.com / utina-diving.com

Comino

Comino Dive Centre (Diveshack)
Comino Hotel
Tel: +356 2134 5671 / 7799 3483 / 2133 8558
info@divecomino.com
www.divecomino.com

Diving Information

Maltese Diving Regulations

Check before you travel

Up to date information can be found on the Professional Diving Schools Association (PDSA) website: www.pdsa.org.mt

At time of writing, the requirements for divers on their next visit to Malta and Gozo are as follows.

Dive centres

Only licensed dive centres are allowed to offer scuba training or other recreational diving services. Visiting instructors can only conduct teaching through a local dive centre. That dive centre will issue you with a temporary instructor card. There is no cost.

Diver permits

Qualified level 2 Instructors (BS EN ISO 24802-2:2014 / ISO 24802-2:2014) visiting who wish to supervise training and/or diving for those less than PADI Advanced, BSAC Sports, CMAS 2 Star or equivalent, must do so through a licensed dive centre.

Instructors must produce proof of certification, third party insurance cover, full diving medical, be proficient in emergency and have safety procedures in place should the need arise.

A Maltese Instructor Permit is no longer needed but a form of photographic identification issued by a local dive centre is required. This must be visibly carried and presented if necessary to any Malta Tourist Authority (MTA) official.

Independent divers

If you intend to dive without a local guide you must hold a PADI Advanced Open Water, BSAC Sports Diver, CMAS 2 Star or equivalent qualification or higher, autonomous diver (BS EN ISO 24801-2:2014 / ISO 24801-2:2014).

An Independent diver is a person qualified to at least 30m. If younger than 15 years old they must be accompanied by an adult.

Dive Leader/guide

A person qualified to PADI Divemaster, BSAC Dive Leader, CMAS 3 star or higher (BS EN ISO 24801-3:2014 / ISO 24801-3:2014).

Must provide a valid medical certificate, have knowledge of the underwater terrain and be qualified to administer emergency oxygen.

Dive leader duties include guiding or organising a group of independent divers, helping to control participants, improving safety but not assessing or teaching skills or knowledge to clients.

Minimum age

There are no restrictions on age unless diving independently *(see 'Independent divers')*. The decision on minimum age will be at the discretion of the instructor or as stipulated by the training agency for those undertaking a diving qualification. Written parental/guardian consent will be required for all divers under 18 years of age. Check with your chosen dive centre on their rules governing age restrictions.

Medical requirement

A simple self-declaration medical statement must be filled in by all divers at their diving centre. This will highlight those people who must seek further medical advice and/or examination prior to diving.

Should the need arise, your dive centre can arrange for a local doctor specializing in diving medicine.

Technical diving

The use of rebreathers, nitrox and trimix are now sanctioned, subject to the normal restrictions of training and experience. Check with your chosen dive centre prior to your arrival.

Diving Information

Wind & Temperature

If you are diving unguided, it is important to be able to assess the conditions.

BFT	Wind speed	Wave height	Description	Sea conditions	Land conditions
0	<1 km/h <1 mph	0m 0ft	Calm	Sea like a mirror, dead calm.	Smoke rises vertically, very quiet.
1	1–5 km/h 1–3 mph	0–0.2m 0–1ft	Light air	Ripples with the appearance of scales are formed but without foam crests.	Direction of wind shown by smoke but not by wind vanes.
2	6–11 km/h 4–7 mph	0.2–0.5m 1–2ft	Light breeze	Small wavelets, still short but more pronounced. Crests have a glassy appearance and do not break.	Wind felt on face; leaves rustle; ordinary vane moved by wind.
3	12–19 km/h 8–12 mph	0.5–1m 2–3.5ft	Gentle breeze	Large wavelets. Crests begin to break. Foam of glassy appearance. Perhaps scattered white horses.	Leaves and small twigs in constant motion; wind extends light flag.
4	20–28 km/h 13–18 mph	1–2m 3.5–6ft	Moderate breeze	Small waves, becoming longer; fairly frequent horses.	Raises dust and loose paper; small branches are moved.
5	29–38 km/h 19–24 mph	2–3m 6–9ft	Fresh breeze	Moderate waves, taking a more pronounced long form; many white horses are formed (chance of some spray).	Small trees in leaf begin to sway; wavelets form on inland waters.
6	39–49 km/h 25–31 mph	3–4m 9–13ft	Strong breeze	Large waves begin to form; the white foam crests are more extensive everywhere (probably some spray).	Large branches in motion; whistling heard in telegraph wires; umbrellas used with difficulty.
7	50–61 km/h 32–38 mph	4–5.5m 13–19ft	High wind, moderate gale, near gale	Sea heaps up and white foam from breaking waves begins to be blown in streaks along the direction of the wind.	Whole trees in motion; inconvenience felt when walking against the wind.
8	62–74 km/h 39–46 mph	5.5–7.5m 18–25ft	Gale, fresh gale	Moderately high waves of greater length; edges of crests begin to break into spindrift. The foam is blown in well-marked streaks along the direction of the wind.	Some twigs broken from trees. Cars veer on road. Progress on foot is seriously impeded.
9	75–88 km/h 47–54 mph	7–10m 23–32ft	Strong, severe gale	High waves. Dense streaks of foam along the direction of the wind. Crests of waves begin to topple, tumble, and roll over. Spray may affect visibility.	Slight structural damage occurs (chimney-pots and slates removed).

BFT	Wind speed	Wave height	Description	Sea conditions	Land conditions
10	89–102 km/h *55–63 mph*	9–12.5m *29–41ft*	Storm, whole gale	Very high waves with long overhanging crests. The resulting foam in great patches is blown in dense white streaks along the direction of the wind. On the whole the surface of the sea takes a white appearance. The tumbling of the sea becomes heavy and shock like. Visibility affected.	Seldom experienced inland; trees uprooted; considerable structural damage occurs.
11	103–117 km/h *64–72 mph*	11.5–16m *37–52ft*	Violent storm	Exceptionally high waves. Small and medium-sized ships might be for a time lost to view (behind the waves). The sea is completely covered with long white patches of foam lying along the direction of the wind. Everywhere the edges of the wave crests are blown into froth. Visibility affected.	Very rarely experienced; accompanied by widespread damage.
12	≥ 118 km/h *≥ 72 mph*	≥ 14m *≥ 46ft*	Hurricane force	The air is filled with foam and spray. Sea completely white with driving spray; visibility very seriously affected.	Countryside is devastated. Boats smashed.

Air and Sea Temperatures

Month	Air High	Air Low	Sea (average)
January	16°c *(60°f)*	0°c *(32°f)*	17°c *(62°f)*
February	16°c *(60°f)*	1°c *(33°f)*	16°c *(60°f)*
March	18°c *(64°f)*	1°c *(33°f)*	15°c *(59°f)*
April	20°c *(68°f)*	5°c *(41°f)*	17°c *(62°f)*
May	24°c *(75°f)*	10°c *(50°f)*	19°c *(66°f)*
June	29°c *(84°f)*	13°c *(56°f)*	22°c *(71°f)*
July	43°c *(109°f)*	11°c *(51°f)*	26°c *(79°f)*
August	44°c *(111°f)*	18°c *(64°f)*	27°c *(80°f)*
September	37°c *(99°f)*	15°c *(59°f)*	26°c *(79°f)*
October	35°c *(94°f)*	10°c *(50°f)*	24°c *(75°f)*
November	28°c *(83°f)*	0°c *(32°f)*	22°c *(71°f)*
December	23°c *(73°f)*	1°c *(33°f)*	19°c *(66°f)*

Diving Information

Tourist Information

English	Maltese
Hi	Hello
Good morning	Bongu
How are you?	Kif int?
I'm fine, thanks	Tajjeb, grazzi
And you?	U int?
Good/ so-so	Tajjeb/ insomma
Welcome (to greet)	Merħba
Good evening	Wara nofs inhar it-tajjeb
Good night	Il-lejl it-tajjeb! /banswa
Thank you (very much)	Grazzi (ħafna)
See you later	Narak iktar tard!
Good bye	Ċaw!
Can I help you?	Nista ngħinek?
Can you help me?	Tista tgħini?
One moment please	Mument, jekk jogħġbok
How much is this?	Kemm jiswa dan?
Excuse me	Skuzi!
Come with me	Ejja mieghi!
Yes/ no	Iva/ le
What's the time?	X' ħin hu?
What's your name?	X' jismek?
Please	jekk jogħġbok
My name is …	Jien jisimni …
Mr…/ Mrs…/ Miss…	Sur…/Sinjura…/ Sinjorina

English	Maltese
Nice to meet you	Ghandi pjacir
You're very kind	Int gentili
Where are you from?	Minn fejn int?
I have to go	Ha jkolli mmur
Happy birthday!	Happy Birthday!
Happy new year!	Is-sena t-tajba
Merry Christmas!	Il-Milied it-tajjeb
Congratulations!	Prosit!
Sorry (for a mistake)	Skuzani
No problem	Mhux problema
I don't understand	Mhux nifhem!
I have no idea	M' ghandix idea
What is this?	Dan x' inhu?
This/ that. Here/ there	Din/ dak. Hawn/ hemm
Me/ you. Him/ her	Jien/ int. Hu/ hi
I need a doctor	Ghandi bzonn tabib
One, two, three	Wiehed, tnejn, tlieta
Four, five, six	erbgha, ħamsa, sitta
Seven, eight, nine, ten	sebgha, tmienja, dis-gha, għaxra
Tea with milk and sugar	Te bil-ħalib u zokkor

N.B. Most locals speak English.

Timeline

circa 3,600 BC	The Ġgantija Temples, the oldest free-standing structures in the world are built, making Gozo's civilization more than 2,000 years older than Egypt's pyramids.
700 BC	Phoenicians established colonies in Gozo, which they named Gwl (or Gaulos). They built the walled town of Gwl (the inner part of present-day Victoria).
550 BC	Maltese islands were swayed under the control of Carthage.
400–500 BC	Archaeological evidence suggests the island was inhabited from the 5th century BC by Sicilian migrants who brought animals plus craft, pottery and agricultural skills.
218 BC	Romans ousted the Carthaginians during the second Punic War. The island was given the status of a Municipium with the right to mint its own coins. The Romans translated the name as Gaudos or Gaulum, and strengthened the town's walls.
60 AD	St. Paul shipwrecked in Malta. Legend has it that the Gozitans heard him preach from Xewkija.
535	The islands come under the dominion of the Byzantines.
870	Islands conquered by the Aglabid Arabs, who gave Gozo its present name Għawdex (pronounced 'Aww-desh'). The citadel was built and the ancient Phoenician and Roman wall that surrounded Victoria was dismantled. The part of the township outside the citadel was named 'Rabat'—the locals still call the main town this today.
1127	Count Roger de Hauteville of Normandy takes possession of Gozo. He allowed the Arabs to remain as long as they paid taxes. The Maltese islands were annexed to Sicily.
1194– 1530	The islands passed to a succession of feudal lords whose sole aim was to extract the highest amount of taxes possible from the local inhabitants. During this time they were ruled by the kingdoms of Swabia (1194), Angou (1266) and Aragon (1282).
1397	Gozitans created the Universitas Gaudisii (a corporation to defend local interests).
1530	The islands passed formally to the rule of the Knights of St. John of Jerusalem. The Order of St. John came to Malta after they lost Rhodes in 1522. They had been there since 1309.
1551	Under the leadership of Sinan Pasha of the Ottoman Empire, the Turks besieged the population of about 5,000 and sold them to slave traders in Libya. Lack of interest in fortifying the citadel and continuous raids by Barbary pirates were the main reasons why no villages developed until the late 17th century.
1660s	The Knights of St. John start to build coastal defences in Gozo and strengthen the citadel walls.
1798	Napoleon Bonaparte ousted the Knights from the islands. However, his rule in Gozo was short-lived—just three months. In September the locals rose up against the French, who surrendered. Gozitans enjoyed a short period of autonomy.
1800	French surrendered to British Admiral Sir Alexander Ball.
1814	Under the Treaty of Paris, the British formally annex the Maltese islands as a Crown colony.
1939	During World War II, Gozo very heavily bombed by the Italian and German air forces. After two and a half years of constant air raids, the bravery, heroism and sacrifice of its people were recognised when King George VI awarded the Maltese people the George Cross.
1964	Malta gained independence from Britain although it maintained its bases on the island.
1974	In December, Malta declared a Republic within the Commonwealth. Five years later the last of the British troops left the island.
1979	31 March—the Union Flag (of Britain) was finally lowered.
1987	The Ministry of Gozo was set up.
1993	14 local councils were introduced on Gozo.
2004	Malta joined the EU on 1 May.

Tourist information is given throughout the book where dive sites are at or near a place of interest. There are also some entries in the Contents (look for the un-numbered items). Here are some of the highlights of Gozo.

Ġgantija Temples, Xagħra

The UNESCO World Heritage listed Ġgantija Temples are one of the most important archaeological sites in the world. Dating from 3600–3000 BC, they precede both Stonehenge and the Egyptian pyramids. The name derives from ġgant, Maltese for giant. Due to its size, the site was commonly believed to be the work of giants, and even a race of giants descended from Noah. The monument consists of two temples and a massive boundary wall.

Salt Pans, Salini

Salt harvesting in Gozo dates back centuries — some of the earliest rough hollows were dug out of sandstone rocks in the Phoenician period. There are over two kilometres of different salt pan systems on the northern coast alone. From May until September they fill with seawater which then evaporates, leaving a white crust. The salt is distributed to local businesses, but it is also sold directly from the pans in small bags. The locals use it especially for cooking, preserving and for making cheese.

Fort Chambray

Designed by military engineer Louis François d'Aubigné de Tigné to replace the Citadel in Victoria as the island's capital. Jacques de Chambray (a Knight of St. John) undertook control of the building work although he died before completion, in 1758. It was the best-defended and provisioned fort on the island, but the intended town was never built. The fort's rich history includes: the locals (with British help) defeating Napoleon Bonaparte's forces; being used as a hospital during the Crimean War; a convalescent home during World War I; a mental hospital and a leprosarium. It is now being redeveloped for tourism and leisure and into luxury apartments.

Fougasse

The 18th century fougasse was designed to fire large quantities of stone at enemy ships. There is some debate about whether or not these truly qualify as fougasses, it seems they may have been a combination of the explosive mine and the mortar. As they had to be cut into solid rock, in Malta the weapon had permanence, solidity, and form not found elsewhere (most fougasses were employed in field defences and earthworks). Gunpowder was placed at the bottom of the pit, then a fuse was fed through a channel in the side. The gunpowder chamber was covered with a wooden lid. Finally, the pit was filled in with a large number of stones or flints. A good example can be seen at Ix-Xatt I-Aħmar.

The Aqueduct

You will drive through the Aqueduct on any journey between Victoria or Għarb and Ta' Pinu, on the way to or from Dwejra. No longer used, the aquaduct is partly ruined but still awe-inspiring. It was completed in 1843 during the British colonial period. It supplied the central water reservoir within the Victoria Citadel with fresh water from Għar Ilma hill in San Lawrence. An obelisk commemorating the arrival of the water supply still stands on the spot of the first reservoir.

Qolla il-Bajda Battery

Overlooking the inlets of Qbajjar and Xwejni Bay is Qolla il-Bajda Battery, built between 1714–1716. Its blockhouses (which also served as accommodation) had holes in their flanks so that musketeers could provide covering fire along its land front. In 1770 it accommodated four six-pounder guns. The main gate was approached by a short flight of steps across a drawbridge. It was abandoned by the British in the 19th century but used as an observation post during World War II. In 1979 it became a bar and later a disco, bringing a number of structural changes. Sadly it is now an abandoned ruin.

The Three Hills

There are several interesting hillocks around Marsalforn. The most famous is Tas-Salvatur (Our Saviours Hill), which has a statue of Jesus on it. Tas-Salvatur is also referred to locally as Tal-Merzuq (Ray of Light) as according to legend (in the 17th century) fire and light was seen coming from it. In 1901 a large wooden cross was erected on its peak, but when Gozo was consecrated to Christ the Saviour in 1904 it was replaced with a stone statue of Christ. This was later replaced by the twelve metre concrete statue which remains to this day. Il-Qolla Bajda (The White Butte) protrudes from the beachhead between Xwejni Bay and Qbajjar Bay, beside the Qolla il-Bajda Battery. It is formed of layers of different clays with a sandstone slab at the top. Il-Qolla s-Safra (The Yellow Butte) is slightly inland of Qbajjar Bay. It has a top section which seems to twist at different angles to the rest of it.

Towers

Gozo has four of the 14 coastal defence towers built on the islands. They could communicate with neighbouring towers — usually through fires on their roofs. They are all worth a visit. The ix-Xlendi Tower is the oldest free-standing coastal watchtower in Gozo, built in 1650. It was designed to defend Xlendi Bay and keep out smugglers, pirates and quarantine evaders. Mġarr ix-Xini Tower (pictured) was built in 1661 and restored in 2000. Dwejra Tower was built in 1652 (restored in 1993) to guard the previously unde-fended Dwejra coast and deny access for anyone not authorised to go to Fungus Rock (see Site 49). San Blas Tower (it-Torri ta' Isopu, or ta' Sopu and Torre Nuova) was built in 1667 and restored in 2006.

A visit to Gozo is not complete without sampling the atmosphere of a festa. Typically lasting three or more days, church and village are adorned with decorations, parades take place, street stalls sell food and there are fireworks displays. The dates given are the local saint's days, which the festa will be held on or near to.

Month	Day	Festi (Feast Day)	Village(s)
February	01	St John Bosco	Victoria
	10	St Paul	Munxar, Marsalforn
March	14	St Gregory	Kerċem
	25	Annunciation	Victoria
May	Final weekend	St Paul	Munxar
June	06	St Anthony	Mġarr, Għajnsielem
	13	Corpus Christi	Għasri
	20	Sacred Heart Of Jesus	Fontana
	24 (Sunday nearest)	St John The Baptist	Xewkija
	29	St Peter and St Paul	Nadur
July	04	Visitation	Għarb
	11	Our Lady of Perpetual Help	Kerċem
	16	Our Lady of Mount Carmel	Xewkija
	18	St George	Victoria
	25	St Margaret	Sannat
August	First Sunday	St Joseph	Qala
	08	St Lawrence	San Lawrence
	15	The Assumption of Our Lady	Victoria
	22	The Assumption of Our Lady	Zebbug
	29	Our Lady of Loreto	Għajnsielem
September	05	Our Lady of Mount Carmel	Xlendi
	08 (Sunday after)	Our Lady of Graces	Ir-Rabat
	08	The Nativity of Our Lady	Xaghra
October	10	Our Lady As Patron Saint	Għasri
	10	Jesus of Nazareth	Xaghra
December	08	Immaculate Conception	Rabat, Qala

If you want to experience authentic Gozitan cooking, ideally you need to eat with locals in their homes. There food recipes have been handed down over many generations and have evolved over the years. Dishes are influenced by all of the cultures which have at one time or another occupied or traded within the Maltese islands.

Aljotta – Maltese fish soup ('Sopop') made with lampuki dorado (fish) stock. It consists of lots of garlic (aglio), onions, tomatoes and very importantly, marjoram.

Bajtra – Prickly pear liqueur made from *Opuntia ficus-indica*, also known as the Indian fig or Barberry fig. The cactus fruit is collected locally between August and September each year.

Balbuljata – A traditional dish made with scrambled eggs, tomatoes, garlic, parsley and seasoning. Other ingredients added are spring broad beans or corned beef. It is eaten with thick slices of fresh bread (Ħobż).

Bigilla – Spicy bean dip or spread on local bread.

Bragoli – Beef rolls. Meat wrapped around a filling of beaten eggs, fresh bread crumbs, parsley and grated cheese. Placed in the oven with fried onions, peas and simmered with red wine.

Brungiel mimli – Eggplant with beef or pork mince, egg and cheese.

Capunata – Made from aubergines, green pepper, tomatoes, oil, onions, garlic, and celery. It is served cold as a light lunch and goes well with lamb or fish dishes.

Fenek moqli ('fenek') – Lightly fried rabbit, simmered in tomato sauce, with peas, potatoes, bay leaves and red wine.

Fenkata – A meal where friends or families meet and rabbit is eaten.

Figolla – Typical Maltese sweets for Easter.

Ġbejna (plural: ġbejniet) – Cheeselets made from goat or sheep's milk, salt and rennet. Ġbejniet niexef (dry). Ġbejniet maħsulin (dry with pepper and salt). Ġbejniet are a key element of many recipes.

Ħobż – Bread. Many bakeries produce a variety of fresh daily bread and traditionally baked products like the ftira, which is a kind of Gozitan pizza flavoured with tomato paste and anchovies.

Kinnie – A soft drink first developed in 1952 by Simonds Farsons Cisk. It is a blend of bitter oranges combined with an infusion from a dozen different aromatic herbs and spices such as anise, ginseng, vanilla, rhubarb and liquorice.

Kisksu soup – Pasta with potatoes, beans and onion with fresh Gozo cheese.

Kwarezimal – Lenten cake, to eat when fasting.

Laħam fug il-fwar – Pork chops and potatoes covered with water, simmered slowly on the hob, together with garlic, parsley, salt and pepper.

Minestrina soup ('sopop') – A mix of seasonal vegetables, legumes and pastas.

Pastizzi – Small savoury cheese (ricotta) and pea cakes.

Prinjolata – Carnival cake, a traditional Maltese dessert prepared especially for the carnivals held in February.

Pumpkin pie and rice – With tuna, olives, capers, fresh mint, salt and pepper.

Qaghaq – Yeast rings.

Qaghaq tal-gulglien – Rings of crisp sesame-covered bread.

Qaqocc mimli – Globe artichokes, stuffed and steamed.

Qara bagħali mimli – Zucchini stuffed with minced meat.

Qassat – Fresh Gozo cheese, broad beans, egg and grated parmesan.

Ravjul – A traditional Gozitan ravioli, served with plain tomato sauce poured on top, a drizzle of olive oil, parmesan cheese and garlic.

Rizza – Sea urchin, eaten with lemon and bread.

Ross il-form – Baked rice, best eaten warm but also delicious cold. It is often cut into squares to be consumed on the beach or taken on a picnic. It makes good party finger food.

Soppa ta' l-armla – Widow's soup, cooked with vegetables, poached eggs and cheesletts (ġbejniet).

Spaghetti – With tomato sauce, garlic and basil or with rabbit sauce and grated cheese.

Stuffat tal-qarnit – Octopus stew.

Timpana – Baked macaroni in a pastry case.

Torta tal-lampuki – Lampuki is the Maltese name for the dorado, dolphin fish or mahi mahi, which is in season from August to November. It can be pan fried with tomato sauce, capers and green peppers but most know it from lampuki pie, made with fresh spinach, onions, garlic, green olives, capers, tomato sauce, olive oil marjoram and chopped fresh mint.

Zalzett – Sausages made of ground pork and flavoured with coriander seeds, black peppercorns, parsley and sea-salt. They are dried and often eaten fresh with Maltese bread (ħobż).

Information kindly supplied by Marthese Grech of Cool Bar cafeteria and snack bar Xlendi Bay.

North

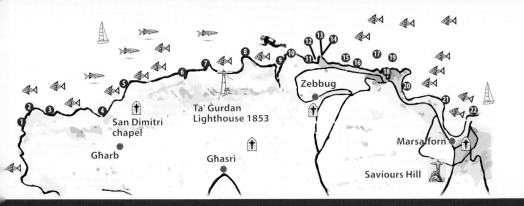

In this area

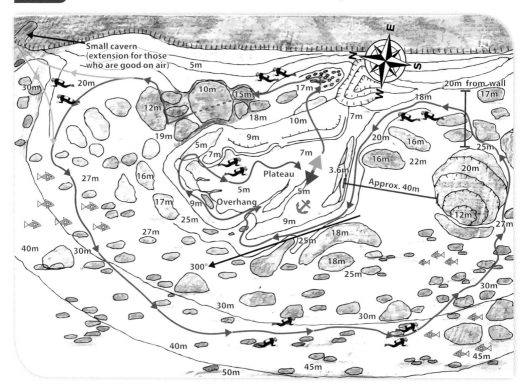

Legend

The cliff of San Dimitri climbs to over 60 metres and is situated on the western point of Gozo. A very popular legend is tied to this site. An old hermit built a small chapel which he dedicated to Saint Dimitri at the edge of the cliff. Many years later Turkish pirates invaded the island and carried away a small boy called Matthew who was the only child of a widow named Zgugina. The mother is said to have prayed to the painting of the saint within the chapel, beseeching him that if her son was returned she would light a lamp, day and night as thanksgiving. San Dimitri came to life and galloped away after the fleeing Turks. He returned with Matthew and the widow kept her promise for many years. One day the land was shaken by an earthquake and the church fell to the bottom of the sea where it is said the oil lamp can be seen — still alight — as a sign of Zgugina's faith.

Dive

From the shallow plateau at 6m where the dive boat anchors, head east towards the cliff wall. Descend the reef to 17m, turning north leading to some large rocks. Following a gully you can go underneath some of the boulders that fill the valley.

On exiting the boulders turn west. This place is renowned for large shoals of truly spectacular fish, so look into the blue for barracuda and around the rocks for groupers and cow bream. When you reach a maximum depth of around 30–40m follow the reef to the south/south-east in a big semi-circle. You might also be able to spot a ray — they are quite often seen at this dive site. A large rock on your left (east) leads back to the cliff wall and the plateau where the boat anchors on the shallow reef.

Do your safety stop here, enjoying the plateau with its colourful marine life. Nudibranch are commonly found, including *Cratena peregrine*.

   This dive can be difficult with surface chop and slight current coming around the corner from the west. It should therefore only be dived in relatively calm waters and a light north or north-east wind.

Nudibranch (Cratena peregrine)

Details
Max depth 6–45m *(20–145ft)*
Duration 30–60 min
Visibility usually 30m+
★ EASY DIVE

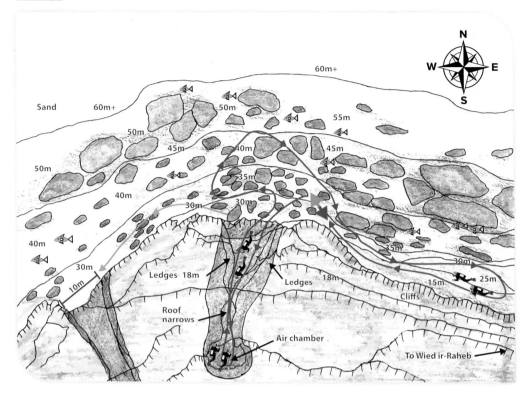

Location

This site is situated on the north-western coast, between San Dimitri and Wied Ir-Raħeb and is accessed by boat. Its local name is Ta Maħsel which means 'the washing place'. Chris Moffitt worked for St Andrew's Divers Cove in the early 2000s. He and others made some exploratory dives and this site is one of the ones they discovered. It is rarely dived.

Dive

Exiting from your boat head straight for the wall following it down to the cavern entrance. The opening is at a depth of about 15m, and it is about 15m wide. The cavern is shaped like a sock. On entering, at 18m look on the ledges on both sides for shrimp and lobster. The walls are covered with colourful sponges of all types, and there are large rocks beneath.

About 60m from the entrance there is a large, dark, vertical shaft or chimney, about 10m in diameter. This takes you from about 15m up to a cavern. There is a large pocket of clean air so you can surface inside if you wish.

On exiting with the cavern floor at 30m, you may wish to venture further out and explore the large rocky area where most of the larger fish will be found. The rocky reef slopes down to 50m with boulders at the bottom. Fish life here includes dusky grouper, moray eels, dentex and Mediterranean lobster.

Turning right (east) the reef wall steps down gradually, a shallower alternative. The boat could follow you along the cliff wall. Turning left (west), there is another 10m wide cavern about 50m away that has not been fully explored as yet, with the sea floor at 30m and roof at 12m below sea level.

Entry point

Greater slipper lobster (Scyllarides latus)

Details
The current normally running from east to west can be strong,
judge this on entry. A torch is essential for the cave.
Max depth 20–50m *(65–165ft)*
Duration 35–50 min
Visibility is usually 30m+
★★ ADVANCED DIVE

3 **WIED IR-RAHEB**

Wied ir-Raħeb or 'the Sacristan's Valley' is a dry gorge that starts several hundred metres inland and ends at the top of the cliff some 25m above sea level. After heavy rain run-off water pours down the valley and over the cliff to spectacular effect.

Exiting the boat, head straight for the wall, following it to see three caverns along the way. The first and third caves are open to the surface and 15 and 25m deep respectively and have walls adorned with colourful sponges and soft corals. The middle cavern is a clean cut doorway in the cliff wall itself and the exit is a roundish window just above it. At the back of the cave is a dark, wide chimney which takes you to the surface and a small air pocket. Rain water run-off forms a halocline *(see Glossary)* here as the salt and fresh water meet. This will distort your vision but is not unsafe.

This site is dominated by massive rocks outside the caverns and it is well worth spending time trying to find creatures.

North

Details

Strong currents flowing west can make this a rather good drift dive.
Max depth 25–50m *(80–165ft)*
Duration 40–60 min
Visibility is usually 20–50m
★★ ADVANCED DIVE

4 GUDJA CAVE (Ta Ċamma caves) BOAT

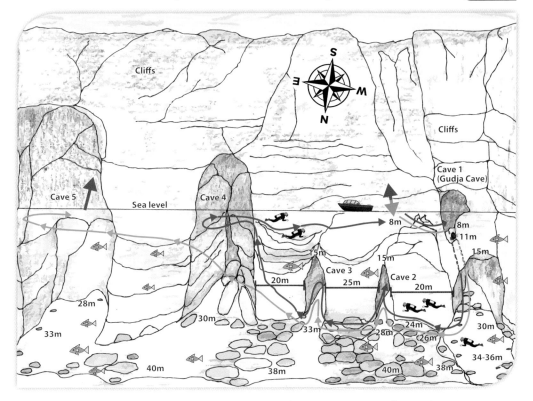

This dive site rarely offers prolific fish life but the underwater scenery more than makes up for it. A sheer cliff towers above the surface then continues underwater and ends at a depth of about 35m. The dive itself is characterised by five caverns collectively called Ta Ċamma. Three of the caves are visible above water and two are completely submerged. The boat will not usually anchor outside.

The dive starts by descending and following the wall until the top entrance to Gudja Cave (in the corner), which is only 8m in depth and about 2m wide. Just a few metres inside the cave floor disappears abruptly, falling to a depth of 30m. This is the entrance or exit, depending on where you wish to start this dive.

Swimming inside from the top hole at 8m the walls inside narrow then open again revealing two inner chambers (which are not overhead environments). You will need a torch on entering the second one.

On turning around and exiting these chambers you will see a massive arch 20m high and to your right the top hole at 8m. This forms a spectacular exit from the cavern at a depth of 30m. Exiting you will see rocks of varying sizes and a slight bank to your right taking you to the second cavern which is set in the reef wall about 20m away. Cave 2 is about 4m wide and 8m high, with a pointed roof and a sandy floor at a depth of 28m. Here, look for brightly coloured anemones. Cave 3, about 25m further along the reef wall, is similar but a little deeper.

At this point you may be getting close to your no decompression limit (NDL), but air and NDL-permitting I normally carry on past the third cave to the large open cavern that is Cave 4. It is about 30m wide and the depth is between 20 and 25m, with steep-sided walls.

The reef bottom with its large rocks is home to groupers while the many fissures, cracks

7

and small holes in the walls offer refuge to a lot more marine life.

Cave 5 is also large and open to the surface, large enough to take a boat. It has steep-sided walls with a rock-strewn bottom and tapers at the end.

Entrance to Gudja Cave (Cave 1)

Details

You will not be able to see all five caves on the same dive unless you have access to a scooter.

Max depth 25–50m *(80–165ft)*
Duration 40–60 min
Visibility is usually 20–50m
★★ ADVANCED DIVE

BOAT

ROY DAVIDSON

Ras il-Hekka is a brilliantly-coloured cavern with an open roof above it — below water it is about 15m deep. There is a steep wall to the right outside the opening which leads to a large submerged cavern, the top of which is at 12m. It is full of colourful corals and the view from the inside looking outwards is breathtaking.

The bottom of the cave entrance is at around 27m with a sand and rock floor and the walls have 'shelves' where all sorts of marine life can be found hiding, from nudibranchs to seahorses. The cave floor is littered with rock and coral fragments — seahorses can often be found amongst these as well as fan mussels (*Pinna nobilis*), heart urchins and forkbeards trying to hide.

Much of the dive can be spent exploring the large cave which does not go very far back and it is not possible to get lost in, as long as you keep your fins off the bottom and don't stir up the silt. If you wish, when you have finished exploring the cave you can swim along the wall outside, and there is a chance to spot stingray, eagle ray, tuna or barracuda.

North

Details
Max depth 10–40m *(30–130ft)*
Duration 30–50 min
Visibility is usually 30m+
★ EASY DIVE

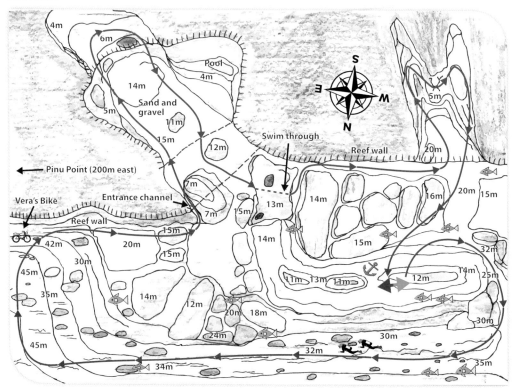

Wied il-Mielaħ (Salty Valley) is located at the end of a rocky inlet on the north coast. It is a cleft within the cliffs, the end of which boasts a natural rock 'window'. The mayor of Għarb's local council, David Apap Agius, addressed the sorrowful state of this picturesque valley by spending €800,000 to improve it in two phases between 2003 and 2011. It became one of 21 European Destinations of Excellence (EDEN) winners. It is now on the tourist map and attracts many visitors each year. This site cannot be dived from the shore even though there are steps which reach down to the water's edge. The dive is easy and can be undertaken in varying ways to suit all levels of qualification.

If your boat anchors on the raised plateau, head west to the end, turning north then east along a vertical reef wall at the depth of your choice. Choose deeper waters for larger fish like dusky grouper, although barracudas can often be seen quite shallow. At the end of the wall boulders appear — many with voids underneath them — eventually leading to the cliff wall. The wreck of an old motorbike known locally as Vera's Bike is at 43m at the base of this wall. It was thrown off the cliff above by an angry father to stop his son using it.

Turning west along the wall, up the rocks and past a small arch at 15m you will reach the first of two caverns. To enter, you can get between a large rock and the reef wall or simply swim over the rock at 7m. The first cavern is wide and long, open to the air above, tapers in at the back, rises slightly and then opens out inside the enclosed area at the back.

As you exit west, on the way to the second cavern about 20m away, a boulder with holes in the top forms a swim-through at 14m. On entering the second, smaller cavern at 20m look to your right where the rock overhangs — bubbles will stream out of the floor below you — and follow this around and up to 10m. After a good look about return to the boat, doing your safety stop on the way there.

Details
Max depth 18–50m *(60–165ft)*
Duration 40–50 min
★ EASY DIVE

Wied il-Meilaħ cavern

From il-Margun

One way to do this dive is to drop off the boat at Il-Margun (which means place of the cormorant) a little to the east *(see Pinu Point on page 22)*. This way you will visit another cavern, and about 25m outside it starts shallowing-up towards the entrance with boulders all around. It is a gentle dive that takes a good 15 minutes. The depth inside the cavern varies due to the rocks on the bottom and it ends up as a narrow passageway with a maximum depth of 4m. You can surface inside and it is large enough for a small boat in calm conditions. Then head west towards Wied il-Miela with the reef wall on your left and finish the dive as before.

Details (From il-Margun)
Max depth 18–40m *(60–130ft)*
Duration 50–80 min — allow at least one hour
Visibility usually 30m+
★★ ADVANCED DIVE

7 PINU POINT (Għar Tal-Margun)

About 290m to the east of Wied il-Mielaħ a spike of rock juts out which is dominated by two large caves that stretch almost to the top of the cliff down to the sea below. This dive is also sometimes called il-Margun and one of the caves you will explore as part of this dive is that mentioned in *Site 6 (see 'From il-Margun')*. The rest of the dive involves going further east, around the corner.

The sloping seabed is completely covered with boulders of varying sizes. Fish life here is not as abundant as one might expect but the topography more than makes up for it. This photo was taken between Wied il-Meilah and il-Margun.

Details
Max depth 10–40m *(33–130ft)*
Duration 40–60 min
Visibility usually 30m+
★ EASY DIVE

North

This dive starts at about 5m on a plateau a short distance from the reef wall that extends approximately 150m to the east. There are two options: either drop down following the reef wall east, or stay shallower following the wall on top of the plateau. If you choose the deeper route, a steep drop-off leads to a seabed littered with boulders and onto two caverns to the east of Forna Point. One is called Għar taz-Zokkor (Cave of Sugar) and there are also lots of smaller ones to the south.

Details
Max depth 10–40m *(33–130ft)*
Duration 40–60 min
★ EASY DIVE

North

9 WIED-IL-GĦASRI TO CAVE OF WIND/CATHEDRAL CAVE (Għar il-Riħ)

An isolated, deep, winding valley cut into the headland and 98 arduous stone steps to get down, Wied-il-Għasri (Valley of the Grape Crusher) is a very picturesque setting. This site includes Għar il-Riħ, which translates as 'Cave of Wind', but it is also known as both Cathedral Cave and Blue Dome.

I would not attempt this site after heavy rain as it silts easily. Prepare your equipment at the top of the stone steps. Not forgetting anything, make your way down to the stony beach at the bottom. Enter the shallow water and to your right look for an impressive old shaft cut through the sandstone rock. Swim out to the 4m mark on the map, admiring the valley walls on both sides.

Descend and follow the valley out and around to your right where gradually the reef slopes away, then suddenly drops to 25m. There are usually many damselfish on the reef wall. Keep right and in front of you you will find the cave entrance at just 5m below the surface with the sea floor beneath you at about 20m. Go inside and surface if you wish, observing a safety stop if required. This will have taken you about 20–25 minutes.

On surfacing you will be in a large, impressive, cathedral-like dome-shaped cavern about 20m in diameter and 8m high with large boulders beneath at 5–12m. It is safe to take off your mask and regulator as near to the entrance there is a crack which allows light and air in. The light also enters from below, turning the water a strikingly vivid blue. At the back there is the bottom of a disused well that I do not advise visiting as it is a cramped space and with surge can be dangerous.

When you are ready, descend and exit over the rocks with the reef on your left, down and around to a patch of sand at 30m. Follow the reef around the column of rock on your left (the top of which is at 14m), up the rock-strewn escarpment and left at the reef wall turning south-east back into the valley. Damsels, moray, cuttlefish and octopus may be seen on the second part (which your computer might log as a separate dive) and may take between 20 and 30 minutes.

CATHERINE & JEAN PIERRE CORNAND

Details
Max depth 6–35m *(20–115ft)*
Duration 35–50 min
Visibility usually 30m+
★ EASY DIVE

10 CAVE OF WHEAT (Għar il-Qamħ)

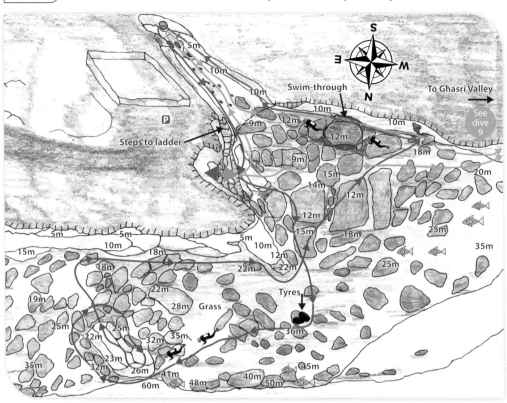

- 5m
- 10m
- 10m
- Swim-through
- 10m
- To Ghasri Valley
- See dive 9
- P
- Steps to ladder
- 9m
- 12m
- 10m
- 12m
- 18m
- 20m
- 9m
- 15m
- 14m
- 12m
- 25m
- 12m
- 15m
- 18m
- 35m
- 5m
- 5m
- 10m
- 5m
- 10m
- 12m
- 25m
- 15m
- 18m
- 15m
- 10m
- 18m
- 12m
- 22m
- 22m
- 19m
- 22m
- Tyres
- 25m
- 28m
- Grass
- 36m
- 25m
- 25m
- 22m
- 32m
- 35m
- 23m
- 45m
- 35m
- 32m
- 26m
- 41m
- 40m
- 50m
- 60m
- 48m

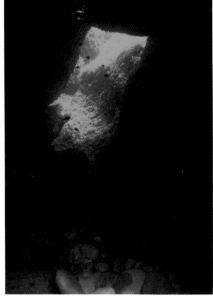

Entering Għar il-Qamħ and the small swim-through just before it

Also known as Ras il-Kanun and Ta Lenk by different dive centres. A ladder and handrail were reinstated in June 2013 after a ten year gap and that re-opened this site for shore diving. This is also an alternative, easier way to get to Wied-il-Għasri (*Site 9*). A 14 minute swim to the west allows access by just following the reef at your desired depth.

The eastern side of Għar il-Qamħ has a nice reef wall and a plateau with a sheer drop off from the north side to 60m. Near the entry point there is a nice, long, part-underwater shallow cave, a small cave and a swim-through at 15m, which offer the novice a great exploration dive.

Entry ladder

Details
Max depth 6–35m *(20–115ft)*
Duration 35–50 min
★ EASY DIVE

BILLINGSHURST CAVE (Għar ix-Xiħ)

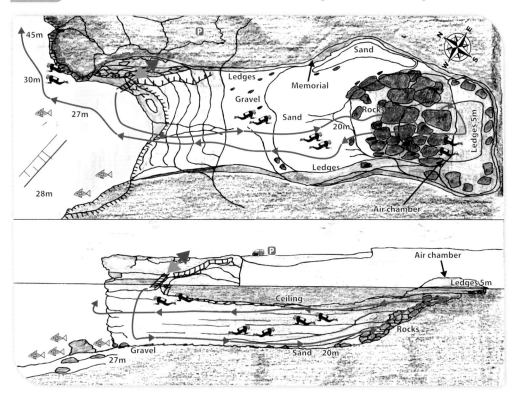

This large cave entrance on the north coast is exposed to the prevailing winds and shows signs of extensive erosion. As you might expect, there is less marine life than in some of the southern caves. Nevertheless, you will still find a variety of coloured bryozoans and algae on the rock walls, starting just below the surface. The gravel bottom under the ladder is 27m deep.

The Billingshurst branch of the British Sub Aqua Club (BSAC) discovered this cave in the late 1980s. The sound created as the waves crash into the outer opening in winter has earned it the nickname Booming Cave. Its local name is Għar Ix-Xiħ meaning 'Old Man's Cave'. It is one of the largest caves on Gozo that is easily accessed by shore. A long tunnel, sometimes called 'The Railway Tunnel' on account of its shape, leads to the back, deep inside the cave.

Park your vehicle at the top, west of Reqqa Point. A short walk down takes you above the entrance via a handrail to the ladder, which was replaced in 2011. Good planning and safety procedures will ensure a safe dive — this cave extends in about 100m; double-check equipment before entry. You will need torches as at the back there is very little light. On descent the 15m wide entrance ensures there is plenty of light initially.

Keep slightly to the right side over gravel for 30m, then for 20m over sand up to a series of boulders that greet you at a depth of 20m. Slowly ascend with the rocks in front of you towards the back where a long ledge at approximately 5m is an ideal place to kneel down and admire the view.

Above the ledge is a chamber and vaulted ceiling about 10m in diameter. The air here is not particularly good to breathe, so I do not usually surface, but instead turn and look towards the entrance before switching torches off. In the darkness a shaft of blue light is clearly visible from just under the ceiling of the cave at 9m. Head back out, keeping shallow. On either side of you there are ledges which are usually filled with the shining eyes of common prawns (*Palaemon serratus*). The view while swimming out is awe-inspiring. It takes about 12–14 minutes to exit slowly.

If time permits visit the memorial — a 10cm (4") rectangular plaque at 17m on a ledge with a plastic flower, often covered with sand — which commemorates the Boxing Day 2004 tsunami. Your options are then to swim to Reqqa point 210m right/north-east, which takes a further 20 minutes; or alternatively, to explore the outside reef walls on either side of the cave entrance.

Details

Overhead environment. Total length of about 100m exceeds recreational limits, so this is not for everyone! It is quite often used for laying lines and training.

Max depth 15–30m *(50–100ft)*
Duration 35–50 min
★★ ADVANCED DIVE

12 SHRIMP CAVE

DR VERA WITTENBERG

Situated on the north coast between Billingshurst Cave and Reqqa Point is a low-cut underwater cave with its entrance at 35m. From entry D on the Reqqa map (*Site 13*) make your way along the reef wall heading south-west for about 60m, gradually getting deeper until the cave opening becomes distinct from the sea floor, rising just a few meters high. The cave soon comes to an end inside, but most of it is actually above you as a shaft ascends with ledges to a sandstone roof at 26m.

You will notice it gets noticeably warmer inside, probably due to groundwater entering from above as a halocline is sometimes present. This is where a body of water of higher salinity (sea water) sinks below less saline fresh water.

Shrimp Cave opens out with ledges all around which provide a home for many of its namesake residents (*Lysmata seticaudata*). They scurry around trying to hide and disappear into the many holes. A torch is essential in this dark area. There is also a resident conger eel and forkbeards are often seen within the cracks near the sandy floor.

The cave can comfortably accommodate up to four divers, but be aware of kicking up too much silt as visibility can be considerably impaired.

On exiting the cavern you have two choices. Turn right (north-east) back towards Reqqa and enjoy the scenery before exiting at B, C or D on the Reqqa map. Alternatively, turn left (south-west) and head towards Billingshurst Cave (*Site 11*) approximately 60m away, exploring the reef wall before exiting at the ladder there.

Details
Max depth 35–50m *(115–165ft)*
Duration 40–55 min
★★ ADVANCED DIVE

13 REQQA POINT

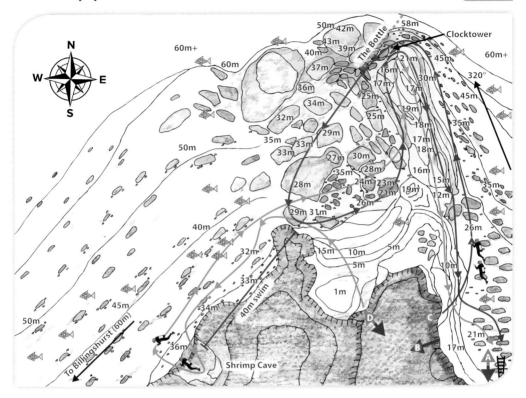

Reqqa is the most northerly point on Gozo, a low curving spur jutting out 30m from the headland. Entry and exit points on both sides can prove difficult — it depends on the amount of swell and personal fitness level, so judge this on arrival.

Take care when walking down as the rocks are jagged — wearing boots is a must. There is a handrail and ladder to the east for your entry/exit (A). Portable toilets are sometimes provided in the summer months.

From the right-hand/eastern entry C, take a giant stride out. It is 20m to the bottom where the diver in the photo on *page 42* is getting in. Descend and follow the curving spur around the reef wall to the 'Clock Tower' — a column of rock that stands proud of the end of the reef wall. This will take you about 10 minutes. Achieve your maximum depth on the way round.

The water here is usually very clear and has an abundance of life. At the end of the reef below the clock tower the reef turns sharply to the south. Follow the rocks in front of you, being mindful of your bottom time. Sightings of large grouper — some over a metre in length — are common amongst these rocks, and include goldblotch (*Epinephelus costae*) and dusky (*Epinephelus marginatus*).

Carry on until you reach the reef wall then turn east, shallower now, which will lead you past a recess to a plateau at 18m. This will take a further 10 min. Here look up the bank to your right and you will see exit/entry D on the western side of the spur. To your left/north you can follow the reef to the top of the clock tower at 14m.

Hanging above the clock tower always gives me a sense of awe, with clear views all around, an impressive drop off and there are often Mediterranean amberjacks (*Seriola carpenteri*) and striped barracuda (*Sphyraena viridensis*) hunting up and down the reef.

North

Turn and follow the reef back along its south-eastern edge towards your chosen exit. Large shoals of cow bream (*Sarpa salpa*) often feed on the bank along the way here. Sometimes a current from the east can be a bit strong to swim against so an alternative is to exit up the bank to D, thus avoiding having to swim around the point.

On reaching exit A, if you have sufficient air, visit the chimney that is 20m or so east. The entrance is 16m deep, 2m high and 3m across, set in the reef wall and is large enough for no more than two divers at a time. Go in and look upwards, ascending to one of the two exits (at 10m and 7m). Be careful not to bang your tank valve as you leave. Turning your body at an angle will help. Then make your way back west to exit A or B.

A rope with knots and a weight is often placed at exit B. To use it hold the end of the rope with one hand, remove your fins, place your hands through your fin straps, grab hold of the rope with both hands and pull yourself out with your legs in front of you.

Entry and exit points: Ladder entry/exit = A; rope exit = B; giant stride entry = C west side entry/exit = D.

Details

The map for *Site 14* shows this location from another angle.
Max depth 18–50m *(60–165ft)*
Duration 30–70 min
★ EASY DIVE

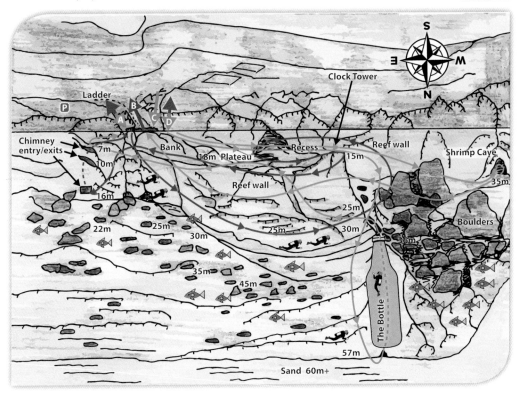

The Bottle is another dive at Reqqa Point, but due to depth — the entrance is at 57m — it should only be attempted by those with special training and experience and must be carefully planned.

The Bottle is a narrow near-verticle chimney. There is a small entry hole following a v-shaped cleft in the reef. You exit at around 35m, at the base of the Clock Tower *(see Site 13)*. After that you can follow any of the options on the map above or on *Site 13*.

Details

The map for *Site 13* shows this location from another angle.
Max depth 18–50m *(60–165ft)*
Duration 30–70 min
★★★ TECHNICAL DIVE

North

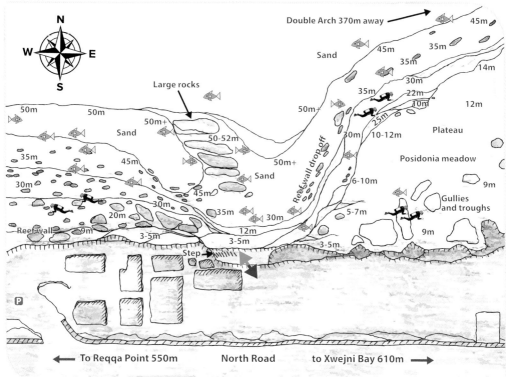

This is a submerged rocky plateau that extends to the east for approximately 200m to Double Arch (see Site 17). Starting at about 2–3m the ledge gradually drops away to 15–17m in depth before descending over the reef walls to 30–40m in steps, then down still further to 50 and 60m on sand with boulders strewn about. There are three possible ways to dive it:

1. Stay shallow on top of the plateau to the east.
2. Turn west or east and drop over the edge of the ridge to get greater depth and then turn back to your entry point.
3. Start at Anchor Reef and make your way to Xwejni Bay — about a 600m swim. This option takes an hour or more so be sure not to go too deep following the plateau, stay between 8–12m.

Sometimes a slight current can come from the east or west, so be prepared to change your plan. I have never found fish life abundant in the shallower depths but there are interesting shapes in the sandstone, which has been worn or carved over many years to quite dramatic effect. There are also larger areas of posidonia grass the further east you go. The reef wall always has something to offer. Over the ridge edge at depths of 10–15m you will find moray eels, damselfish and groupers.

North

Details
Max depth 18–50m *(60–165ft)*
Duration 40–60 min
★ EASY DIVE

16 THE WASHING MACHINE (Ta Buġħas)

This is a shallow but very pleasant dive. The site gets its name from the action of the sea in winter as the water swirls around like a washing machine, making holes in the rock below. The *Site 17* map shows the route. Enter the water and turn west and you will immediately find an 8m to 12m plateau with patchy rocks and posidonia grass. Irregular channels in the sandstone rock, possibly made by freshwater running off the land and formed over many centuries stretch for 200m or so to the west. These interesting rock shapes can harbour much marine life — investigate closely. The reef wall on your right/east also offers many hiding places for octopus and small fish. This is a relaxing and easy dive for the less experienced. Seahorses have been found here along with moray eels, garfish, cuttlefish and many other marine species.

Details

Note: Be careful not to step in the salt pans when walking to and from your entry/exit — these are still in use.
Max depth 6–15m *(20–50ft)*
Duration 30–60 min
Visibility usually 30m+
★ EASY DIVE

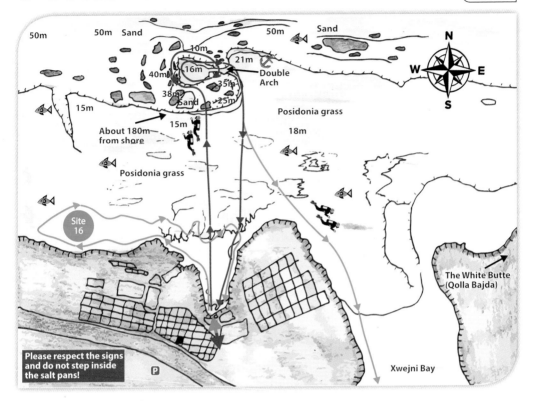

Double Arch or (Twin Arches), is located some 180m offshore, north of the Washing Machine *(see Site 16)*. Be prepared for a long surface swim out and conserve your air for the return. Alternatively, you can do this dive from a boat, which can be easier — ask your dive centre if they are planning a trip.

To help you find your descent point look towards the land while swimming backwards. Keep bearing north until you reach the edge of the reef. To your left is the statue of Christ that will move behind a building *(see Transits for Double Arch on page 48)*. Keep the salt seller's door in view then descend to the reef at 15m. Turn right into the reef bowl.

Passing a patch of sand below you and a few large rocks, Double Arch will be on your right, but follow the reef top at 16–18m all the way around to the left, choosing your depth. Coming back to the other side of the arch, look to the north and see that it drops away gradually with some rocks and sand, very often large dusky grouper, moray eels, dentex and Mediterranean lobster can be seen here at 45–50m. Go through and explore both of these magnificent arches which are covered with sponges and soft corals. Make your way to the top at 21m where there is a good chance of seeing barracuda in their hundreds, this will take about 15–20 min.

After looking around the arch go to the top and take a bearing south over the fields of posidonia grass, gradually ascending until you reach the Washing Machine. Bear in mind that there may be a mild current from the east or west on the return journey. Alternatively, you could follow the reef left/east and then south and exit in Xwejni Bay. This will take you a further 20–25 minutes from the arch thus giving you a total dive time of approximately 40–55 minutes.

North

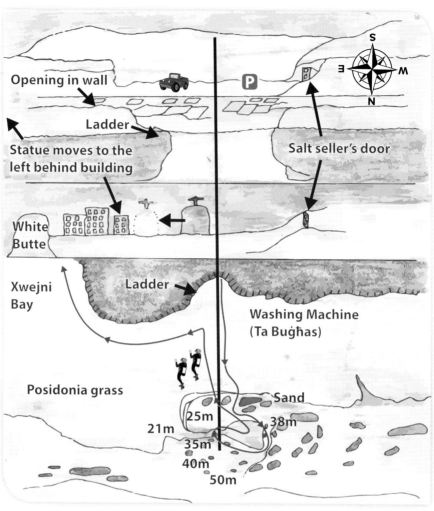

Transits for Double Arch

Details

A mild current from the east or west sometimes slightly sways you off-course, so be prepared to adjust your swim. If currents from the east or west are strong consider an alternative site.

Max depth 15–50m *(50-165ft)*
Duration 40–60 min
Visibility is usually very good at 20–40m
★★ ADVANCED DIVE

Mediterranean moray (Muraena helena)

Double Arch

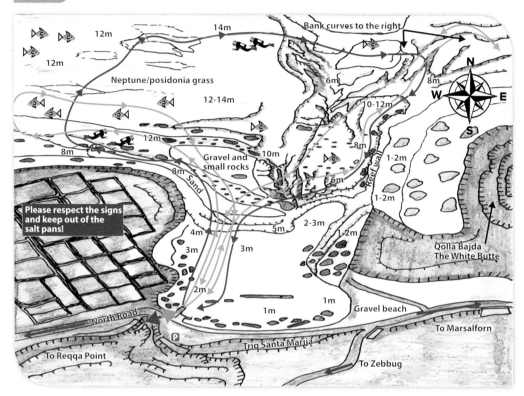

Xwejni Bay is situated between Qbajjar Bay and the Washing Machine on the north road (Triq Santa Marija) approximately 1.5 km from Marsalforn. Park on the road by the bay where there is a handy wall for briefing and kitting up. Toilets and a cafe are placed here in the summer months.

Make your way to the concrete boat ramp that has a handrail leading to the entry/exit point and a pier that extends out about 12 metres. There are three options: Right (blue), left (green) or the square (red) route which I will describe here.

Square route

The entry depth is about 1.5m. Descend and swim out/north 40m to a bank that gradually slopes to not more than 5–8m. Many small fissures and gullies eventually lead to a gravel and pebble seabed. Slightly to your right/east follow a 6m reef wall for about ten minutes. You will gradually get deeper until the wall starts to diminish and curve to the right at 10m.

Before you get to the end of this reef keep a sharp lookout on the gravel bottom for prehistoric shark teeth. I have found many different sorts over the years and it adds interest to your dive. At this point turn west and swim for ten minutes across the posidonia grass. Look out for pipefish, cuttlefish and spiny crabs, there is even the occasional sighting of amberjack and barracuda hunting in the blue.

Turning south, make your way to the reef wall. You may get as far as the Washing Machine *(see Site 16)*. If so look in the fissures for moray eels, octopus and blennies. Rare species I have seen here include the slipper lobster, turtle and seahorse.

Follow the wall back east to complete the dive where you started, so making a square pattern that should take about 40–50 min. This is an easy slow dive with time to explore.

Rusty blenny (Parablennius sanguinolentus)

Details

Currents from the east or west may be present and if strong consider an alternative site. A strong north-westerly wind is not good for this site.

Max depth 6–15m *(20–50ft)*

Duration 30–60 min

★ EASY DIVE

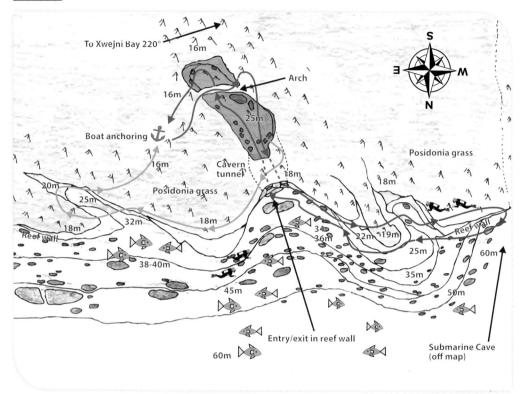

Transits

This dive site lies about 150m offshore from the north-eastern side of Xwejni Bay. To shore dive it using the transits given in the photos, swim out inline with the White Butte and line up the large boulder on the beach with the building behind. To your left the hill will slowly move behind the Qolla il-Bajda Battery building *(see page 17)* the further you swim out. At this point look down to the reef drop off at 16m and you should see two large holes in an area surrounded by fields of posidonia grass meadows.

Alternatively swim to the furthest part on the north-east corner of the reef from Xwejni Bay on a heading of 40° and swim underwater for about 15 minutes until you see the two holes near the reef edge.

Dive

You will quickly realize that this used to be a cavern — the reef wall collapsed inwards creating a narrow bridge or archway between the two holes. Diving down to its exit hole at 30m, look above the cavern to its vaulted ceiling and two narrow horizontal cracks slightly to your left at 21m. Carry on down and exit at 32m at the bottom of the reef wall. Outside the sandy/rocky bottom goes on gently down to 50–70m with large rocks in the distance.

From outside, looking back to the reef from where you have just exited, notice how the wall and openings resemble a face with two eyes and a mouth.

To your right/west there is a small sloping valley and beyond a massive cavern called Submarine Cave with its entrance at 25m and bottom at 47m. This should not to be attempted lightly or without appropriate equipment.

Alternatively, turn left following the reef wall to a crack a few meters away, turning around to go back to the arch and then take a bearing of 220° to Xwejni Bay or return to your waiting boat.

Barracudas are often seen here as well as large grouper between the rocks below you. Often you get a glimpse of amberjacks hunting, and have a look in the walls for lobster.

From the arch head back in a southerly direction, finally exiting in Xwejni Bay.

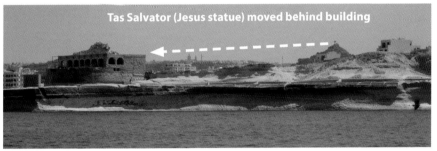

Transits looking to shore

North

Details

Note: Good air consumption is essential, or do not try to complete the entire dive in one go.

Max depth 15–50m *(50-165ft)*

Duration 40–70 min

★★ ADVANCED DIVE

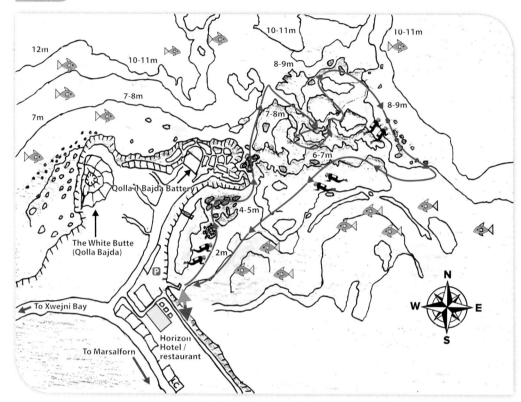

This stretch of coastline has good bathing and snorkelling opportunities, and some very easy diving. Qbajjar Bay is accessed from in front of the Horizon Hotel and has a pebble and rock beach. The turning to the Qolla il-Bajda Battery (see page 17) is slightly hidden from the main road. Straight after taking it, turn sharp right down to the Horizon Hotel and park.

Facilities at Qbajjar include the Chez Amand restaurant — a nice place to have lunch, dinner, or drinks and conversation. The bay is made up of patchy sand, posidonia grass meadows, rocks and boulders. It is a nursery ground for many varieties of marine life including blennies, bream, gobies, garfish, wrasse, tripplefins and octopus. It also has other nice flora and fauna, plus a few arches to swim through.

Dive

From the slipway head out slowly at 40–45° in shallow water for 14 minutes, about 100m. At a depth of 4–5m the top layers that make up the reef structure have fallen away making swim-throughs, arches, overhangs and holes. I find these great fun.

You will be roughly below the Qolla il-Bajda Battery at this point and you can usually see the smooth curved top of the reef wall on your left as you make your way out of the bay. A mixture of colourful bryozoans and soft corals adorn the walls. The sea floor is a mix of sea grass and sand with pockets of small stones.

Eventually you reach the outer reef another 30m or so away that drops down to no more than 8m, with sparse vegetation and large fields of posidonia in the distance.

After following the wall for a short distance start making your way back into the bay on a rough heading of 240°. Keep slightly to your right (250° or 260°) and you will be in the bay within five minutes or so.

Qbajjar Bay

Striped blenny (Parablennius rouxi)

Details
Max depth 2–10m *(6–33ft)*
Duration 40–80 min
★ EASY DIVE

21 SANTA MARIJA BREAKWATER

Found on the eastern side of Marsalforn Bay, this shallow site is used by many dive centres for training or check dives. It also serves as a good bimble for the novice or experienced diver who wants to have a relaxing dive. The sandy seabed is interspersed with medium sized rocks and patchy beds of posidonia grass.

Details

Max depth 2–15m *(6–50ft)*
Duration 30–60 min
★ EASY DIVE

Rock goby (Gobius paganellus)

Għar Qawqla is to the western edge of Marsalforn Bay and has a pillar of sandstone rock that stands about 3m tall. Locals and tourists alike use it as a platform to jump into the sea.

The 'forn' of Marsalforn may derive from the word 'forna' which was used by Gozitan fishermen to refer to a cave hollowed out by the sea (*see page 58* for full explanation). There are several of these in Marsalforn, but by far the best-known is Għar Qawqla 'the cave at the steep hill'. Until the middle of the 20th century this rock was still connected to the land, like a smaller version of the Azure Window. This one eventually fell into the water, just like that most famous arch did in stormy weather in 2017.

Dive

Enter the water on the right side of this rock and dive to a maximum depth of about 10m. I don't advise going any deeper as there may be currents and being too far off is not a good idea without boat cover. Stick to the shallows looking amongst the rocks scattered across the seabed for the many tiny inhabitants which have set up home including small octopus, tiny eels, gobies, shrimp, blennies and other small colourful fish.

Details

Max depth 2–10m *(6–33ft)*
Duration 30–60 min
★ EASY DIVE

MARSALFORN BAY

This bay located on the north coast lies between the hill-top towns of Xagħra and Żebbuġ and forms part of the locality of Żebbuġ. Marsalforn is the most popular tourist resort on Gozo with a number of hotels, restaurants and bars. It has a small, sandy beach and along the rocky coastline there are a number of swimming spots with ladder access.

The bay is quite developed compared to other resort areas on the island — many multi-storey buildings have been built in recent years, most of them along the western side. Many of these places are available for short and long-term rental during the summer months. There is also a hotel near the beach side of the bay close to the waterfront.

The smell of fresh seafood and local vegetables cooking in the evening always seem to hit the spot after a day of diving, especially when accompanied by an exquisite local wine.

Marsalforn dates back to Roman times. Until the 16th century it was the most important port in Gozo, importing food from Sicily and taking passengers travelling to or from Licata and other continental ports. The name derives from more than one source. 'Marsa' is an Arabic word meaning 'port' or 'bay', but there is disagreement about the origin of the 'forn' part. In Maltese it means 'a bakery', but it seems unlikely that one would have been built in an area with such a small population. Like other Gozitan ports, the name might come from a type of ship. In that case 'liburna', an Illyrian type of ship, which became 'livurna' in Greek and 'lifurna' in Arabic would explain it. Alternatively, it may be connected to 'forna', a word used by Gozitan fishermen referring to a cave hollowed out by the sea (see Site 22).

By the late 16th and early 17th century Marsalforn had grown in importance to the extent that the Knights considered abandoning the old Citadel and building a new town overlooking the port. Local hostility ensured the plans were never realised, with protests that they were too poor, could not afford the extra taxes and that disruption caused by moving their homes from Rabat would be too great. When Mġarr harbour was developed, Marsalforn lost its importance — for several centuries remaining a quiet fishing village inhabited by a small community of fishermen and their families. You will be able to see the colourful Maltese fishing boats (see 'Luzzu' on page 107) either floating in the bay or on land undergoing renovations.

Saint Paul (the Apostle) was shipwrecked in Malta and legend says that it was from

North

Marsalforn that he embarked for Sicily on his way to Rome. The story is evident in the village emblem, which consists of a viper encircling a sword. This references an incident whereby Paul was unharmed after being bitten by a venomous snake. The village church called 'Saint Paul Shipwreck' is dedicated to the memory of Paul's departure from Marsalforn. Originally constructed in the 14th century, this church has been rebuilt many times — the foundation stone of the present building was laid in 1730. The feast of the village saint is celebrated on 10 February each year *(see 'Village Festas' on page 18).*

MARSALFORN
MALTA

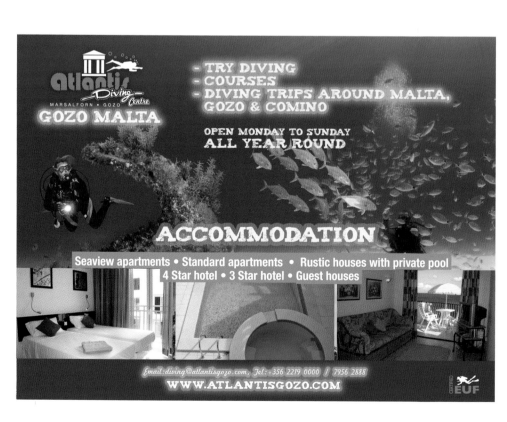

South-east

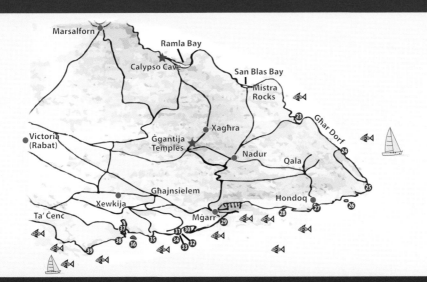

In this area

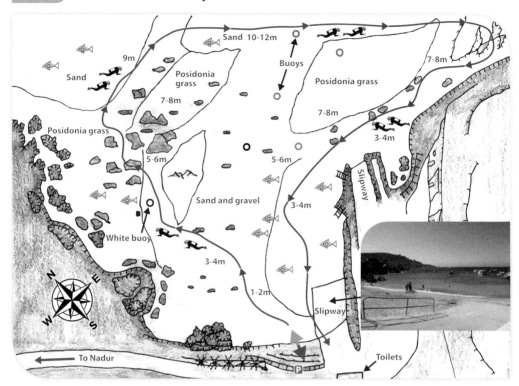

This site is very rarely dived as it is a bit off the beaten track. From Victoria follow the back road left around Nadur centre (Tigrija Street). Turn left at the sign saying San Blas and Dahlet Qorrot. In a short distance the road forks — take the right fork and follow the road to the harbour. The bay is sheltered except in a strong north-west wind (check the swell). It is suitable for beginners and has public toilets (open in summer only) but no other facilities.

There is no phone box and normally no mobile phone signal until reaching the top of the hill. The harbour is primarily a picturesque fishing port and usually quiet. Often there is a lot of Neptune grass (*Posidonia oceanica*) interspersed with rocks and sand.

Dive

The dive itself is a giant circle. Starting at the beach or slipway head toward a white buoy or the tip of San Blas headland north. You should come to a few large rocks at 6–8m in depth, one of which has a small arch. Then head east with a patch of sand on your left and large patches of grass on your right. Eventually it will just be sand with very little grass. Curving around to your right you may see a linear 4–6m bank on your left, this is your deepest part, at about 10–12m. Turning south at this point and slowly rising with fissures and tufts of grass interspersed with sandy areas, you will eventually see the reef in front of you. Follow it around past the boat slipway and back into the bay. I have seen large rays, turtle, octopus, cuttlefish, nudibranch and many different kinds of fish at this site.

I have included this dive, as if you are self-guided and have time on your hands you could explore the walks and scenery here as well as enjoying an easy dive. For training this site offers much: a gradual sloping beach on to sand and gravel with visibility usually 10–20m or more.

Public toilets (summer only); Nudibranch (Thuridilla hopei)

Details
Be aware of any boat traffic.
Max depth 2–16m *(6–50ft)*
Duration 30–60 min
★ EASY DIVE

24 QALA ANCHORS/THE OLD QUARRY

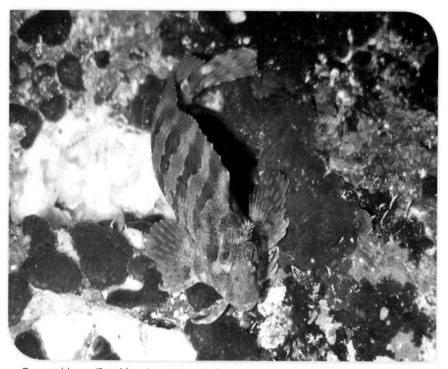

Tompot blenny (Parablennius gattorugine)

Slightly north of Qala Point and a large quarry on the land lies Qala Anchors, or the Quarry Dive. With a starting depth of just 6m the reef gradually slopes down to 30m to sand and posidonia grass.

This site has a nice healthy reef and on the way down, at 20m, amidst the jumble of rocks across the slope there are a few large anchors which have been lying there since the 1960s. The contours are home to a variety of bream, octopus, cardinalfish, wrasse, moray eels and damselfish. Rarely dived.

Details
Max depth 6–30m *(20–100ft)*
Duration 30–60 min
Visibility usually 20–30m
★ EASY DIVE

At the most easterly point on Gozo is a dive not prone to silting as the sand is quite course and pebbly, so visibility is usually very good.

The boat will anchor inside a sheltered inlet away from any prevailing northerly winds. Posidonia grass is dotted all around on entry at 6m, sloping down to 15-30m. The area has rocks scattered about, forming a habitat for an abundance of life. Rarely dived.

Details
Max depth 6–30m *(20–100ft)*
Duration 30–60 min
★ EASY DIVE

South-east

Ornate wrasse (Thalassoma pavo)

26 THE OATH ISLE (il-Ġebla tal-Ħalfa)

Situated on the east coast, opposite the Isle of Comino, lies the picturesque setting of the Oath Isle. In 2002, the Malta Environment and Planning Authority (MEPA) recognised il-Ġebla tal-Ħalfa as a Site of Scientific Importance (for ecology).

Blue Water Dive Centre can offer this as a shore dive. It is a short walk from the end of a narrow road, and they will pick you up in Hondoq after the dive *(see Site 27)*. Small boats shelter here from strong north winds but it is open to occasional east and westerlies.

Dive

The inlet is about 2-6m deep and 60m across with ridges and furrows intermixed with small boulders, ideal for snorkellers and divers alike. On the southern side the rocky floor gently slopes away deeper with scattered boulders and patchy posidonia grass. Explore the southern deepest side first, then head north into the sheltered bay.

This rarely dived area makes for a relaxed, easy boat dive.

Details

Max depth 2–25m *(6–80ft)*
Duration 30–60 min
★ EASY DIVE

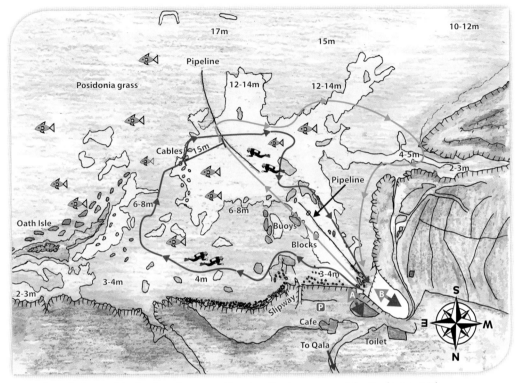

Apart from being an ideal swimming zone, Hondoq Bay is renowned for its diving, with crystal clear waters that make it very popular for beginners, especially in the warm waters of the summer. The bay can be accessed from the village of Qala and lies opposite Comino, with spectacular views. It is sheltered from north-westerly wind and has toilets and a café. You can also hire a boat to take you to Comino's Blue Lagoon a short distance away. This is a lovely small beach, half sand and half small pebbles. The nearest dive centre is Blue Waters Dive Cove. The small church overlooking Hondoq is known as Il-Madonna Tal-Blat (Saint Mary of the Rocks). When in rough weather the priest couldn't cross to Comino, the islanders were able to follow the service across the water.

The pipeline shown on the drawing carries water to Comino. It is usually teaming with marine life including flying gurnard (*Dactylopterus volitans*), cuttlefish (*Sepia officinalis*), gobies, blennies, wrasse, bream and damselfish. This is a good training site and also a good bimble for the experienced wishing to have a relaxing morning or afternoon of diving. The word bimble means simply to amble without real aim and doesn't that just sum up what you're on holiday for?

Dive

This site can be dived several ways, and I am sure Franco of Blue Waters can show you more than I could. I usually follow the pipeline to the end. It runs for 260m at approximately 150°. Then I turn 90° to the left or right for a few minutes, returning by heading north-east or north-west. The only problems can be in the height of summer with boat traffic and amount of people swimming around the beach area. Swim lines are put in place to cordon off areas for swimmers but they are also useful for diver training.

I once saw a spiny seahorse here in just 6m of water — a rare and delightful find to make

South-east

amongst the weed. Well-camouflaged, they are most often found in shallow water, and could be seen at most of the dive sites mentioned in this book including the Blue Hole *(see Site 53)*, Ras il-Ħobż *(Site 53)*, Xlendi Bay *(Site 44)* and most importantly at Mġarr ix-Xini *(Site 37)*. More information can be found at the back of this book *(see 'Diver Guidance for Seahorse Safety' on page 166)* — you may be able to help gather vital information on them.

DAVID RAWLE

South-east

Details
There are two entry/exits: A = ladder; B = beach.
Max depth 2–16m *(6–50ft)*
Duration 30–60 min
★ EASY DIVE

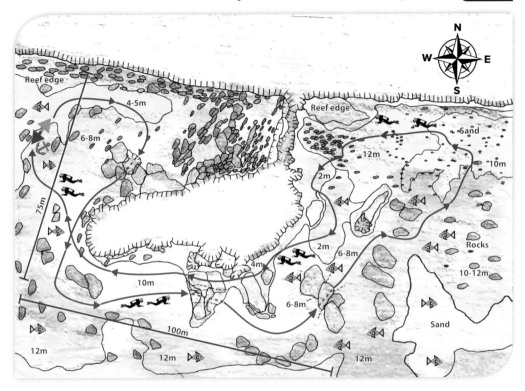

Situated on the south coast between By the Harbour Reef *(Site 29)* and Hondoq lies a rock that stands away from the reef wall. This is a very easy boat dive, perfect for the novice or experienced diver. This site is also known as il-Gebla taċ-Ċawla and Mġarr Rock.

Dive

Starting on the west side at 5–6m go east and then under two large rocks heading south-west. Keeping the reef wall on your left, swim around to another swim-through on the side of the reef wall. Still heading eastwards follow the wall still further to yet another tunnel of rocks at 7m.

On exiting the tunnel, in front of you will be a sandy patch. On reaching it, turn left. The reef wall should now be on your right shoulder.

Marine life is quite abundant at this site with small wrasse, bream, goby and tripplefins.

Details

Max depth 2–15m
Duration 40–60 min
★ EASY DIVE

South-east

Mġarr Rock

Saddled bream (Oblada melanura)

Spectacular scenery overlooking Malta and Comino is the sunny setting for this rarely dived site with an average depth of only 9m. Parking is situated in the top car park in Mġarr by the ferry, below Fort Chambray. Using the 26 steps at the end of the car park, walk down to a pebbly beach. Underwater the landscape is strewn with small and large rocks which provide hiding places for a variety of small fish. Colourful marine plants shimmer as the sun's rays penetrate the water's surface. Entering the water check for current — if there is any, swim out against it to your desired depth, following the reef down. Use your compass to head back towards the shoreline in a circular pattern.

Sand smelt (Atherina hepsetus)

Details
Max depth 2–15m
Duration 30–60 min
★ EASY DIVE

South-east

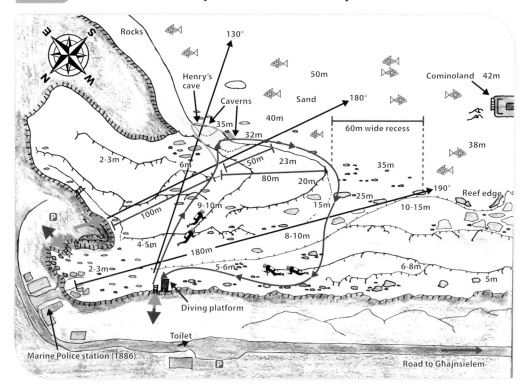

Location

On the Rabat-Mġarr road opposite the parish church of Għajnsielem, a secondary road (sign-posted 'Wrecks') leads down to a secluded bay known as ix-Xatt l-Aħmar or Red Bay. The name comes from the reddish brown colour of the soil on the terraced fields falling towards the sea. Għajnsielem Local Council have improved the facilities here and they now include benches, decking, portaloo toilets and better accessibility to the area.

Although secluded, ix-Xatt l-Aħmar lies within sight of the Guardiola (guard post) of Fort Chambray on the hill to the east. Sunrise and sunset are particularly charming here. The building in the middle of the bay is a former Marine Police Station built in 1886 which had fallen into disuse by 1923.

Dive

This is a safe diving location with easy entry and exits courtesy of two ladders. It is especially popular when north and north-easterly winds render other spots unsuitable as it is quite sheltered.

One of my earliest underwater experiences was in Red Bay when after a great dive we ended up by the diving platform. Under a large rock there was the biggest common octopus I had ever seen with lots of small stones around it. We played a game of me removing some of the stones gently, and the octopus retrieving them with its long arms. I had to go, leaving it to form a wall of stones with one of its big eyes looking at me all the time. It was a most amazing experience. My only wish at the time was that I had a camera — and this is an ideal spot for one. Suffice to say aquatic life is usually very good here with moray eels, cow bream, parrotfish, scorpionfish, pipefish, damsels and cuttlefish.

South-east

If you get as far as the reef edge on the left there are two small caverns, one at 35m and one 15m away at 32m, they aren't big but they aren't dived often and are worth a look inside. You will see sponges, soft corals, sea anemones, beautiful peacock worms and often slipper lobsters too. Unusual spots here include a sea hare (*Aplysia fasciata*) — a sort of reddish brown slug — and a John dory, a wonderful sight.

OCEANFOTO.CO.UK

Don't use the diving platform!

Red scorpionfish (Scorpaena scrofa)

Details

The diving platform is not a safe entrance for scuba. Under the water there is a large boulder that will not hurt the local kids who are usually there as they don't descend deep enough but a 100kg diver with 8kg of lead and 30kg of other equipment will surely end up in hospital, thus his holiday is blighted somewhat. Although isolated incidents, there have been accidents.

Max depth 2–50m
Duration 30–60 min
★ EASY DIVE

South-east

73

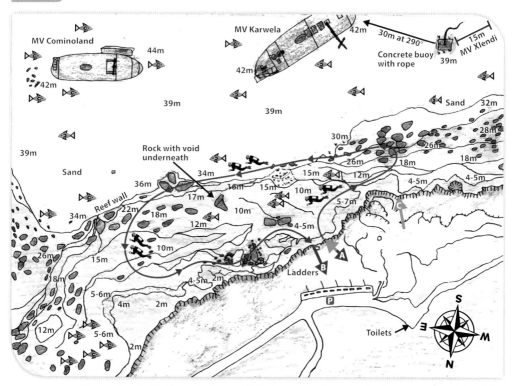

The reef at Xatt l-Aħmar is fun and full of opportunities for the less experienced, both for honing skills and learning new ones. It is also full of life to keep you occupied with all kinds of marine species resident here. From the car park walk down to a gully on the right side of the ladder and there is a short wall, you can sit there and put your fins on. Some prefer using the shallow steps to the left, carved from the edge of the rock by the waters edge. I tend not to giant stride as the water is shallow, but twist as I hurl myself out so the tank hits the water first, especially if protecting a camera. Alternatively, there are two ladders (B on the map), although I only use them for entry if a client needs to because of a disability. In summer with many divers trying to use them to exit it can cause frustration.

Dive

Descend to 4–5m and turn to your right. The reef gradually slopes off and 30m away you will find the edge. Follow this down to your desired depth. Then turn left/east along the wall — it is about 180m long and quite vertical, with the bottom ranging from 28 to 36m.

Just under half way along, look to your right for the wreck of the Karwela which will be about 45m away from you. Carry on along the wall for about ten minutes — it has many cracks and fissures providing homes for moray eels and cardinalfish. Along the top of the reef at 18m there is a large rock supported by a smaller one at one end, which forms a void underneath. Here, turn in a northerly direction, slowly swimming back up to the reef wall at 5m. Look for *Elysia timida* which is only 1cm in length and is a species of sacoglossan sea slug, a marine opisthobranch gastropod mollusc. It feeds on *Acetabularia acetabulum*, a form of green algae, and also *Padina pavonica* commonly known as peacocks tail.

Turning west, follow the reef shallow and back to the ladder exit. A small torch is useful to look under rocks and fissures.

Briefing at the car park

Elysia timida, a sacoglossan sea slug

Portable toilets are placed near the car park here in the summer

Details
Max depth 2–36m
Duration 30–60 min
★ EASY DIVE

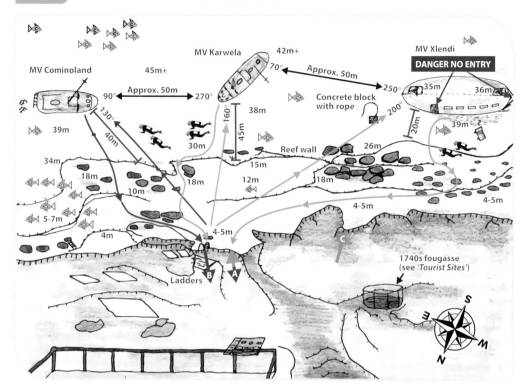

History

The *MV Cominoland* was commissioned in 1941 in England, built by Phillip & Son of Dartmouth as a mine layer and delivered to the British Royal Navy in 1942 as *M6* (*Miner 6*). She had a length of 34m, width 8m, draught 3.6m and weighed 263 tons.

In the 1960s she was sold to E. Zammit & Sons Malta and rebuilt for ferry services within the Grand Harbour at Valletta. She had a capacity of over 400 passengers plus ten cars. Fitted with two General Motors six-cylinder diesel engines with one screw she became the *Minor Eagle*. Renamed *Cominoland* in the 1970s, she continued as a ferry until in 1980 she was renamed *Jylland II* after a rebuild for day cruises in Valletta. Captain Morgan Cruises then purchased the vessel and from the early 1980s she served to take tourists around the Maltese islands, once again named *Cominoland*. She was eventually scuttled at Xatt l-Aħmar in 2006 as an artificial reef in a project part-financed by the EU and lies in an upright position.

Dive

Swim out from the ladder on a bearing of 130° until you can just see the edge of the reef below, or to the marker buoy (only in summer). Stay shallow on the swim out, then on sighting descend onto the wreck.

The top of the wheelhouse is at 30m. You will see window openings from bow to stern. From the bow enter along one of two corridors at 34m which lead towards the stern. A square hole on the deck at the stern is where the engine was, with a winch in front of it.

There is a doorway exit on the port side and the stern has a large opening with a ladder (sharp edges) on the outside leading to the top deck at 32m. Or you can descend here to

South-east

the propeller which is at a depth of 38–40m.

Heading along the top deck, you will come to the smoke stack before rising another 2m to the wheelhouse and mast. From there make your way back to the reef on a reciprocal heading of 310° with no less than 100 bar in your tank. Use the ladder as your exit after your decompression/safety stop in the shallows.

JACEK MADEJSKI

JACEK MADEJSKI

South-east

Details

Deep dive — depth/decompression training essential.
Recreational divers should only attempt one wreck per dive.
Max depth 30–45m
Duration 35–60 min
★★ ADVANCED DIVE

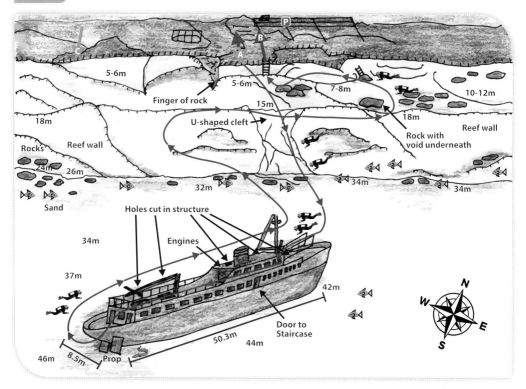

History

See also the map for *Site 32*. *MV Karwela* started life in 1957 as *MS Frisia II*. Built by Jos. L. Meyer, Papenburg, she had twin diesel engines, was 8.5m wide, 50.3m long and weighed 495 tons. She was owned by A. G. Reederei Norden-Frisia. She was renamed the *Nordpaloma* from 1978 and owned by Sagittarius Reederei Beate-Karoline Wilk, Lübeck-Travemünde. She came to Malta in 1987, bought by Mira Towage Ltd Valletta to serve as a ferry with an 800 passenger capacity. Captain Morgan Cruises Valletta took her on from 1992, renaming her *Karwela*. She was sunk at Xatt l-Aħmar in 2006 as a diving attraction.

Dive

Navigating from the ladder will bring you slightly too far east of the bow, so from entry point A swim out to a U-shaped cleft at the reef edge. From there, head on a bearing of 160° at 10–20m deep—the wreck's white and blue paint is covered in a fine layer of weed, darkening it and making it difficult to see from the surface.

From the bow there are two main decks visible. The top deck has five windows and two doors, the lower has two doors. Using the top deck doors you can go in. A few metres inside at a depth of 32m a staircase in the centre will lead you down to the middle deck at 35m. The staircase goes down another level but it is not necessary to do so. A door between the staircases will reveal both engines below you (this is a small space). Turning towards the stern, the middle deck opens out with windows on both sides and two large holes in the deck above.

The stern exits are two doors and a window at 37m. Go over the stern to look at the propellers if you wish—decompression limit permitting—then go on to the top deck.

Make your way to the fallen mast, past the smoke stack to the forward mast. Leave for the reef with a minimum of 100 bar in your cylinder. This has not been planned as a decompression dive but it could easily be one. You will have about 12–20 minutes on the wreck with no deco.

Holes cut in Karwela deck

Inside the Karwela

JACEK MADEJSKI

Karwela staircase

CLAUDINE MARTIN LE COQ

Approaching the wreck

Details

Deep dive — depth/decompression training essential.
Max depth 30–45m (the top of the mast is 28m)
Duration 30–60 min
★★ ADVANCED DIVE

34 **XLENDI FERRY**

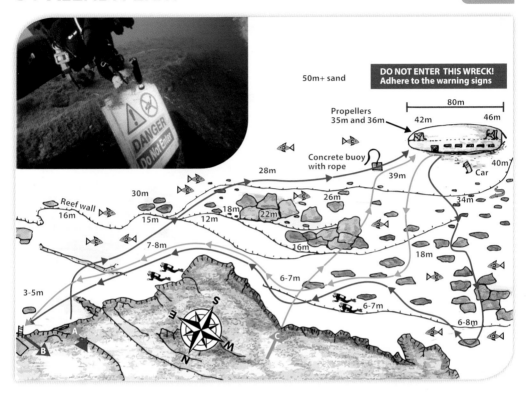

History

Launched in 1955 at the Helsingor Vaerft in Elsinore, Denmark, she was completed in June of the same year and started her ferry career as the *Helsingor*. She was renamed *Royal Sheeba* in 1987, and again to *Borgshorn* in 1988. She was bought by the Gozo Channel Co. Ltd. in 1990 and they changed her name to *MV Xlendi*. She was a roll-on, roll-off ferry, so had propellers at both ends. She weighed 1123gt, was 80m long, had a beam of 12m and was 23m tall. When she stopped operating in 1997 *Xlendi* was handed over to the Gozo Tourism Association to scuttle as an attraction for divers. She became Gozo's first artificial reef when she was sunk in November 1999. However, wind pushed her off the selected position and she hit the reef and sank upside down on sand in 42m of water.

Dive

Entering the wreck is banned as the interior is corroding, so please adhere to warning notices around the vessel. Either enter the water at A and head 200° to the edge of the reef, or enter at C, then proceed on a heading of 180°. C is preferable as it is closer to the wreck, so you can conserve some air. Descend and stay shallow, following the reef down for 3–4 minutes. On the sand below you will see a large concrete block with rope floating up from it — 15m from this block is the *Xlendi's* propeller, at 35m. Follow the hull along its length to the other propeller at 36m, then down to the cargo doors at 40m. Double-back with the reef on your left going past the car. That will take about 15–20 minutes.

On leaving the wreck turn left up the reef. Often amberjacks and barracuda hunt there amongst the rocks. Slowly rise up the reef in a north-easterly direction to the top at 6–7m and back to the exit ladder at B.

Propellor

Part-buried car

Details

Deep dive — depth/decompression training essential.
Watch your air, depth and decompression limits as time
seems to go very quickly.
Max depth 35–45m
Duration 40–60 min
★★ ADVANCED DIVE

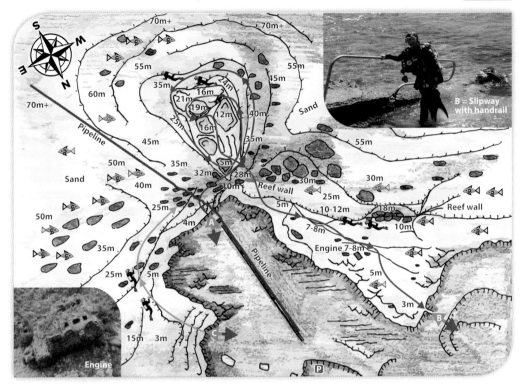

B = Slipway with handrail

Ras il-Ħobż is situated between Mġarr ix-Xini and Xatt l-Aħmar on the southern side of Gozo, down one of two roads past the heliport leading to the waste water treatment plant. It is a rocky, steep, uneven road to the bottom, so the parking area at the top may be more suitable. There are no facilities on site and phone signal is patchy.

The shallow inlet and pipeline are clearly visible but not the pinnacle of rock — or Ħobż — which lies some 40m from the headland. Ħobz means bread — the pinnacle is sort of bread-shaped. Many consider this site more suitable as a boat dive and it can get quite busy in summer with the odd boat from Malta here too.

Dive

I normally enter at the end of the pipeline (A) and exit in the inlet (B) but you can do this any way you feel comfortable — you can also enter and exit in the same place, or enter and exit from the beach to the east (C). Assess conditions on arrival.

From the pipeline entrance follow the reef down to the gap between it and the pinnacle of rock at 28m. Then spiral around the rock choosing your deepest depth — circle it from the left or right, making your way steadily to the top at 9m. There is sometimes a current flowing east at the bottom and north at the top, this may help you to decide where to exit.

Both on the pinnacle and in the blue, this place is usually teaming with life such as barracuda, Mediterranean lobster (*Panulirus elephas*), Mediterranean moray (*Muraena Helena*) and groups of two-banded sea bream (*Diplodus vulgaris*) at the top. There is also an array of small nudibranchs including *Cratena peregrine* and *Flabellina affinis*, so be careful where you put your hands — not that you should be touching anything anyway!

Once at the top and with no less than 100 bar in your tank, head in a northerly direction to the reef wall. Follow it around north-north-west, going past the old engine into the

South-east

83

inlet for your exit. On the way back look out for cuttlefish (*Sepia officinalis*) and octopus (*Octopus Vulgaris*) in the cracks and fissures.

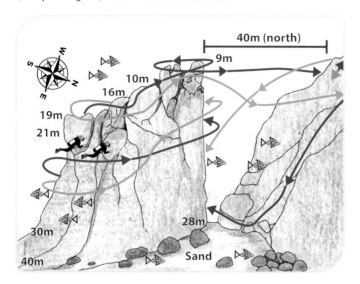

Details

Emergency services may have difficulty evacuating a casualty from such an isolated spot.
Road is in a bad state of repair.
Max depth 6–110m
Duration 40–80 min

★ EASY DIVE ★★ ADVANCED DIVE ★★★ TECHNICAL DIVE

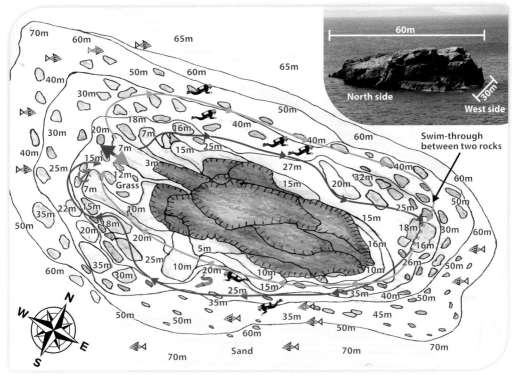

This free-standing rock is found offshore along the south coast in the mouth of Mġarr ix-Xini, 400m from the defence tower and 230m from Ras il-Ħobż. I have dived this site from the shore before but it is normally a boat dive. It is a long swim from Ras il-Ħobż, and would require there to be no current at all. It is an interesting dive at varying depths.

Fessej Rock is a column of rock which rises 15m out of the water. It is 60m long and 30m wide. On the eastern side it plunges vertically — the seabed below is 50m plus. The rock is exposed to certain amounts of current and surge but can still be dived in a light north-westerly wind with minimal swell.

Dive

There is no average depth of the dive as such, you can do this as deep as your training allows or simply bimble along shallow, all the way around. The western side is usually the start as it is the shallowest part and a boat can anchor there. However, most drop off and come back, depending on wind direction and speed. The dive is a simple case of descending down and doing a whole circumference of the rock by heading in a clockwise or anticlockwise direction. Those wishing to not go so deep could stick to the western, shallower part.

On your descent turn to your left (north), this leads you down past large boulders where big grouper, dentex, jacks and barracuda can be sighted along with tube worms and lobster. A little further around there is a tunnel on the north-east side at around 20m.

The south-eastern side is the deepest and darkest part, but leads to a bank where as you shallow up the scenery starts to change with light coming from the south-west. You will see colourful overhangs and crevices in the wall that are home to small fish and octopus, and large rocks to your left. Eagle rays have been spotted here many times as they prefer living in the open ocean rather than on the sea bottom.

Defence tower — It-Torri ta' Imgarr ix-Xini (1661)

Fessej Rock, west side

Details
Max depth 6–70m *(20–230ft)*
Duration 40–60 min
★ EASY DIVE
★★ ADVANCED DIVE (depth dependent)

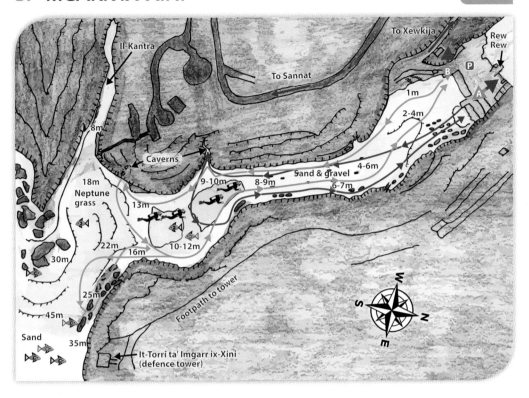

Location and history

Mġarr ix-Xini is at the end of a long winding valley named Il-Wied Tal-Ħanżir (The Valley of the Boar) accessible from Xewkija and Sannat. Recent excavations here have yielded wine presses from the Phoenician and Byzantine eras. The rock-cut huts are thought to be at least 2000 years old and the beach was once a lot further back than it is now.

Mġarr ix-Xini is reputed to be the harbour used by the Knights of St John's galleys. In July 1551, under the orders of Suleiman II of the Ottoman Empire the Turkish pirate Dragut invaded here and used the bay to carry approximately 5,000 inhabitants off into slavery. They were taken to Tarhuna Wa Msalata, in northern Libya.

The valley entrance is still overlooked by It-Torri ta' Imgarr ix-Xini — a tower constructed by the Universita in 1661 to guard against smugglers, pirates and invaders *(see photo on page 86)*. The walk from the bay to the tower on the restored ancient footpath is worth the effort if you have the time.

Mġarr ix-Xini has a small, secluded, pebbly beach. It is a perfect spot for swimming and snorkelling and has one of the best fish restaurants on the island — Rew Rew, run by Noel and Sandra. The bay (and restaurant) was a location used in the 2015 Angelina Jolie and Brad Pitt film *By the Sea*. A hotel was built on the north-eastern side for that film, but it was just a set and was dismantled. Portaloo toilets are put here in summer for the general public.

Dive

I prefer to enter the water on the left-hand side of the slipway (A) as at the end of it you can sit down to put your fins on before surface swimming out. The bay is quite shallow for the first 30m or so.

South-east

Slightly over to the right-hand side, descend and swim for about 250m, gradually getting deeper until you reach the first cavern. This is not an enclosed space but be aware of how many divers enter. It is about 12m wide, with a sandy bottom that rises tapering to an S-bend in the rock near the back, 20m inside. Fresh water run-off mixes with sea water here to form a halocline *(see 'Glossary')*.

On exiting, turn right and follow the wall towards the second cave 70m away at a depth of 13m. Alternatively, head north-east for 60m to the other side of the bay. From there you can either turn right and head towards the large rocks at 25m on your left; or turn left and slowly follow the reef wall back to the beach approximately 260m away.

It is possible to see seahorses here but please *see page 166* for important information on how to avoid stressing them should you come across one on your dive.

JACEK MADEJSKI

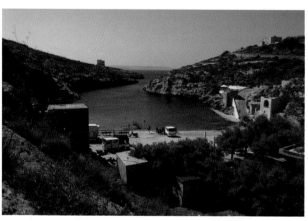

Details

Extreme caution: boat traffic, anchors dropping in summer and sheer numbers of people can make this site hazardous.
Max depth 2–25m *(6–80ft)*
Duration 30–80 min
★ EASY DIVE

South-east

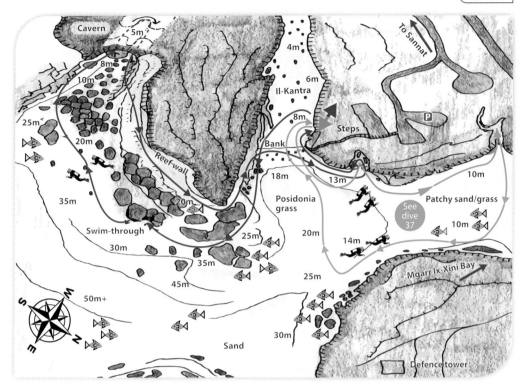

Location

Ta' Ċenċ can be found through Sannat square — left of the church where it forks, keep left until the road ends on a stone track. To your right about 150m along the track stands a small dolmen, a megalithic tomb with a large flat stone, laid on upright stones. In the distance stands Xewkija church which boasts the third largest unsupported dome in the World and is dedicated to St. John the Baptist. Follow the long winding road to Il-Kantra, an inlet with beautiful scenery overlooking Mġarr ix-Xini and with Fessej Rock in the distance looking like a black iceberg.

Dive

Parking in the top car park, prepare your kit and walk down the 96 steps to the water's edge. There is usually a ladder but just to the right of this is a shallow ledge for entry and exit. Descend in 6–8m of water and follow the reef on your right down a slope. This ends at 25m and will take 5–6 minutes.

Go around the large rocks until a sandy area becomes visible on your left, then go in-between them. At 27m, on your right, there will be a small tunnel through the rocks that comes out onto the sandy bottom at 30m.

Carry on along the sand right until you come to some rocks that rise up to a solid wall in front of you. Follow the wall to the top where at 7m in a crevice you will see a hole 1.5m wide which leads to a cavern at the back through which yet another hole appears. Go through and ascend to your right to see your bubbles break at the surface. Then head for the light, looking down at your buddies below you. In the cavern you might find a halocline (if there has been recent rainfall), a large conger eel and sometimes there are thousands

South-east

89

of small rock prawns (*Lysmata seticaudata*), especially around March/April.

On exiting you must have at least 100 bar in your cylinder. Then just follow the reef shallower, keeping it on your left, back into Il-Kantra. You could swim to the cavern to the north, air permitting *(see Site 37)*.

Explore the sand — seahorses, stargazers, common stingrays, Mediterranean moray, sea bream, damselfish, scorpionfish, octopus, tub gurnard, flying gurnard and weavers can all be found here.

Streaked gurnard (Trigloporus lastoviza)

Details

Access is via a gate and path which is part of the Hotel Ta' Cenc & Spa — please be considerate to hotel guests and staff. The gate is only open from 10am–4pm. The bar/restaurant and facilities, which are part of the hotel, are for paying customers only. The restaurant, like the gate, is only open from 10am–4pm.

There are no public toilets here.

Max depth 8–35m *(25–115ft)*

Duration 40–60 min

★ EASY DIVE

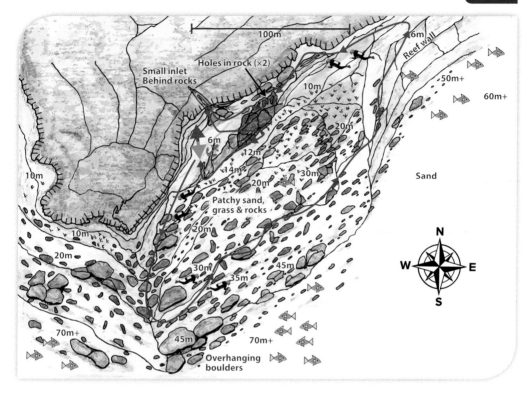

Map labels: 100m | Holes in rock (×2) | 6m | Reef wall | Small inlet | Behind rocks | 10m | 50m+ | 60m+ | 6m | 20m | 12m | 14m | 30m | Sand | 10m | 20m | Patchy sand, grass & rocks | 20m | 10m | 20m | 30m | 45m | 35m | N W E S | 70m+ | 45m | 70m+ | Overhanging boulders

Location and conditions

West of Mġarr ix-Xini and east of the Ta' Cenc cliffs, Ras in-Newwiela is at the most southerly point of the Island of Gozo. It has spectacular vertical cliffs plunging 100m-plus into the clear blue sea. It is sheltered from the north-west but there can be current from the east and sometimes it rips strongly towards the west. There are three small archways and normally a large amount of fish life, so this dive site offers excellent photographic opportunities.

Dive

From the wall make your way south-west — there is a steep undulating drop-off that mimics the cliffs above. Some areas are covered in boulders, offering the opportunity to spot grouper and other shy predators. Octopus and moray eels are common and their lairs can be pinpointed by the shell and crab debris which litter the foreground.

After setting your maximum depth, turn to your left/north-east, following a rocky slope with a small patch of posidonia grass. This eventually drops away to reveal a plunging reef wall that carries on into the distance. The sandy bottom starts at about 45m and drops away to depths of over 60m.

Ascending shallower, turn back south-west towards your waiting boat. There are two small holes through a slither of rock which protrudes from the reef wall. You will be able to swim through one of the holes — it is easily negotiated by divers — the other is slightly too small. It is created by a large boulder leaning against the wall.

Damselfish are found here, mostly juveniles which are royal blue in colour, also colourful algae, cnidaria and bryozoans on the rocks. Deep, by the overhanging rocks you may see large groupers.

South-east

CATHERINE & JEAN-PIERRE CORNAND

Details

Visibility usually very good, 30–50m not uncommon.
Max depth 6–70m+ *(20–230ft)*
Duration 40–60 min
★ EASY DIVE
★★ ADVANCED DIVE (on depth only)

South-west

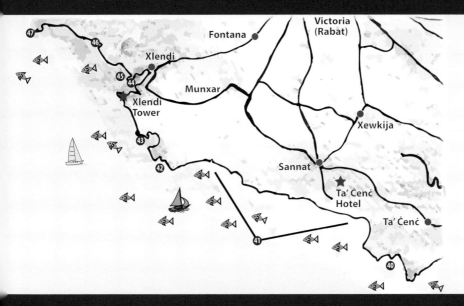

In this area

40 TA' ĊENĊ REEF

Birdlife

The Ta' Ċenċ cliffs are some of the highest on Gozo, at up to 150m tall. They hold one of the largest breeding colonies of Cory's shearwater in the Maltese islands. Shearwaters usually mate for life and return to the same nesting site year after year, when the female will lay just one egg. During the breeding season between March and November, every evening just before sunset, shearwaters gather on the sea in their hundreds — it is an amazing sight.

Dive

Your boat will anchor on a plateau, the top of which starts at about 12m and drops down to the west at 17m. Descend southwards to very large boulders at 30–40m which reach a sandy bottom that slopes off to deeper water. Keeping the reef on your right, swim all the way around and eventually ascend back to your boat. There is a good chance of seeing rays here.

Details

Max depth 10–35m *(33–115ft)*
Duration 30–60 min
★ EASY DIVE

41 SANNAT CLIFFS

History

Ta' Sannat is a small village with tall cliffs and rich fauna and flora. It is known for its ancient cart ruts and prehistoric remains. These include the Borġ l-Imramma Temple and three dolmens (a roughly-shaped horizontal limestone slab supported on three sides by blocks of stone standing on end). It is a perfect walking destination.

Dive

This long stretch of coastline has much to offer divers: large and small rocks interspersed with posidonia grass, sand beds , overhangs, caverns and some unique underwater topography. The high cliffs above plunge down into the blue sea, then slope gradually off into the distance. This largely unspoilt and under-dived area presents an opportunity to find large amounts of pristine marine life over a stretch of coastline measuring about 2,500m (1.5 miles) long.

The depth along the bottom of the cliffs varies from a few meters to about 20m. Some 70m away from the wall the rocks gradually diminish to a sand and shell bottom with one or two rocks scattered about in the distance. The depth at this point is about 30–35m. A further 40m or so and the shelf drops down a further 20m before it levels out at about 70m.

A typical static boat dive would start from the cliff edge in about 8m of water. Planning a square pattern profile, return back to your boat, making your safety stop along the reef edge. Alternatively have the boat drop you off and follow you along the coastline as far as depth, time and air permit.

Things I have seen there include damselfish (*Chromis chromis*), Mediterranean moray (*Muraena helena*), horned octopus (*Eledone cirrhosa*), common cuttlefish (*Sepia officinalis*), greater slipper lobster (*Scyllarides latus*), common stingray (*Dasyatis pastinaca*), and many small varieties of wrasse including the ornate wrasse (*Thalassoma pavo*) and large shoals of cow bream (*Sarpa salpa*).

South-west

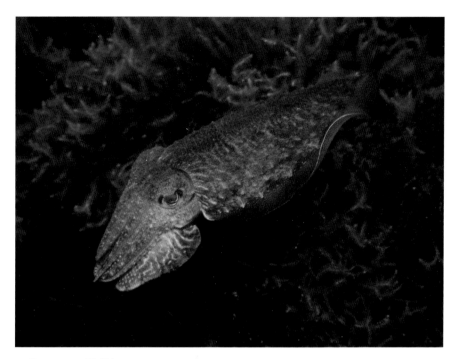

Common cuttlefish

Details
Max depth 5–35m *(15–115ft)*
Duration 30–60 min
★ EASY DIVE

Prehistoric dolmen

Bajjada Point in Munxar is the perfect boat dive that has something for all levels of diver. It is a good choice when the wind is blowing from the north or east. It features two caverns that you are able to surface in should you need to.

Dive

Your boat should moor on a large rock in 6–7m of water. After entering the water follow the reef to the south-west, down to your desired depth. The reef below mirrors the cliffs above water. Then, turn east and follow the rocky slope across, usually I do this at about 20–30m deep for about 60m. Make your way up to a grassy area at 15m. You will now see a large cavern that extends about 50m into the cliff. Swim to the back, it is not dark. There, at 6–7m, a large piece of rock protrudes and it has two holes in it — see the picture above. Swim out on the opposite side of the cavern with no less than 100 bar.

Now cut back across the entrance, heading west whilst admiring the view of the open water. After finning 60m, on your right a shallow cavern will appear with a small swim-through under a rock, just inside its entrance. When you have finished in this cave return to your boat outside.

Details

Max depth 6–40m+ *(20–130ft)*
Duration 30–60 min
★ EASY DIVE
★★ ADVANCED DIVE

South-west

Bajjada Point (smaller cavern). The small swim-through is under the large rock on the left of the picture.

43 DAWRA TAS-SANAP

BOAT

Situated south-east of Xlendi Bay, this dive site offers a spectacular reef drop-off, boulder slope, cavern and a tunnel. Depending on whether or not there is any surge, boats will usually anchor on the shallow reef near to the cliff face.

Underwater, the walls arch around you and reach depths of 10–18m. The area is characterised by patches of posidonia, sand and large rocks that slope seawards. On entry, head for the reef wall in a south-westerly direction. Following the wall you will reach the edge of the reef that leads down steeply to a sandy bottom at 50m. In this area there are some large rocks and most of the time you can find shoals of saddled bream (*Oblada melanura*), cow bream (*Sarpa salpa*). You will often also see hunting dentex and large groupers within and around the rocks.

Swim close to the vertical wall and ascend slowly up a rock-strewn escarpment to 25m. You will pass a linear wedge of rock close to the reef wall that has voids beneath it. This area — including the rocks all around — is a haven for many forms of life.

You will come to a cavern at 18m in the side of the reef wall on your right/north-west. It has a big semi-circular entrance and a sandy bottom full of rocks covered with colourful sponges. It goes in about 20m or so and is perhaps 30m in length and full of light.

On exiting, to your right you will see a large tunnel about 15m across. Go past it and circle the edge of the reef, coming around to the other end of the tunnel that starts on a ledge at about 10–12m. Enjoy the wonderful sight of the tunnel and the sunlight coming from behind you. Stop at the entrance to look on the right-hand side for the nudibranch *Flabellina affinis*, then swim straight through, heading east. Some fallen rocks have formed voids that a diver might be able to squeeze through.

Follow the wall back on your left out of the tunnel above the cavern and back to your waiting boat.

South-west

99

CLAUDINE MARTIN LE COQ

Sea slug, nudibranch (Flabellina affinis)

Details
Max depth 10–50m *(33–165ft)*
Duration 40–60 min
★ EASY DIVE

XLENDI BAY

The picturesque small fishing village and harbour of Xlendi Bay is engulfed by high cliffs and surrounded by the villages of Munxar, Fontana and Kerċem. At the boatyard stands a white statue of the apostle Saint Andrew, patron saint of fishermen, which dates from the late 1800s. The village motto is *Navium Tutela* meaning 'protection for vessels'.

The name Xlendi probably derived from *Xelandion*, a type of Byzantine vessel which may have used the port. A tomb dating from Punic-Byzantine times was found at St Simon Point in Xlendi Valley, cut into the rock two metres below the edge of a rocky spur known locally as Tortoise Rock. The round open tomb can be seen from the road leading to Victoria.

Xlendi Valley starts at Fontana, continuing from the Lunzjata Valley and Wied l-Għawdxija and collects all the rain that falls on the adjacent villages. This in turn flows down to Xlendi Bay and into the sea. It is one of the few places where the protected Maltese freshwater crab can be found.

St. Catherine of Siena Cave (Għar ta' Santa Katarina) in the bay is said to be where Grand Master Perellos would have lunch in 1699. He also received the chiefs of the island who came on boats to pay him homage and present him with gifts.

Xlendi Tower, inaugurated by Grand Master Juan de Lascaris-Castellar in 1650 and completed in 1658 was built to prevent pirates landing within the bay. In 1961 amphorae and anchors were recovered nearby and are displayed in the Natural History Museum in the Citadel in Victoria. They are believed to have belonged to a Roman merchant ship that was wrecked. Diving is now restricted there.

In the 17th century St Simon Chapel was built at St Simon Point. The bishop ordered that a stone cross be carved in the rocks — this can still be seen today even though the chapel has long gone.

In the bay there is a cave which shelters fishermen's vessels. To the right of that there are some steps that lead to Carolina's Cave. You walk down into it through a gate that was once locked so that the Dominican sisters could bath in private. It is named after their

South-west

benefactor Miss Carolina Cauchi. In 1868 she built a small church dedicated to Our Lady of Mount Carmel which is now the only chapel in Xlendi. It has its feast in September.

There is also a cold war flour mill that has been renovated and opened as a museum next to the Church (see www.munxar.gov.mt/flour_mill.html).

There are many bars and some excellent restaurants to suit all tastes, most offer free Wi-Fi. There is ample free parking and public toilets. There are three diving centres in Xlendi — Moby Dives, St Andrews Divers' Cove and Utina Diving College.

Tower

Site of archaeological interest — diving restricted

Posidonia grass and sand

35m

35m

37m

30m

25m

Crock rock

14m

180°

9m

15m

Old ladder

10m

12m

7m

10m

Sand 15m Gap

6m

Wied il-Kantra

9m

9m

4m

Concrete blocks

11m

9m

Debris

3m

Overhead

8m

9m

8m

6-7m

Approx. 60m

7-8m

P

Bench

4m

6m

5m

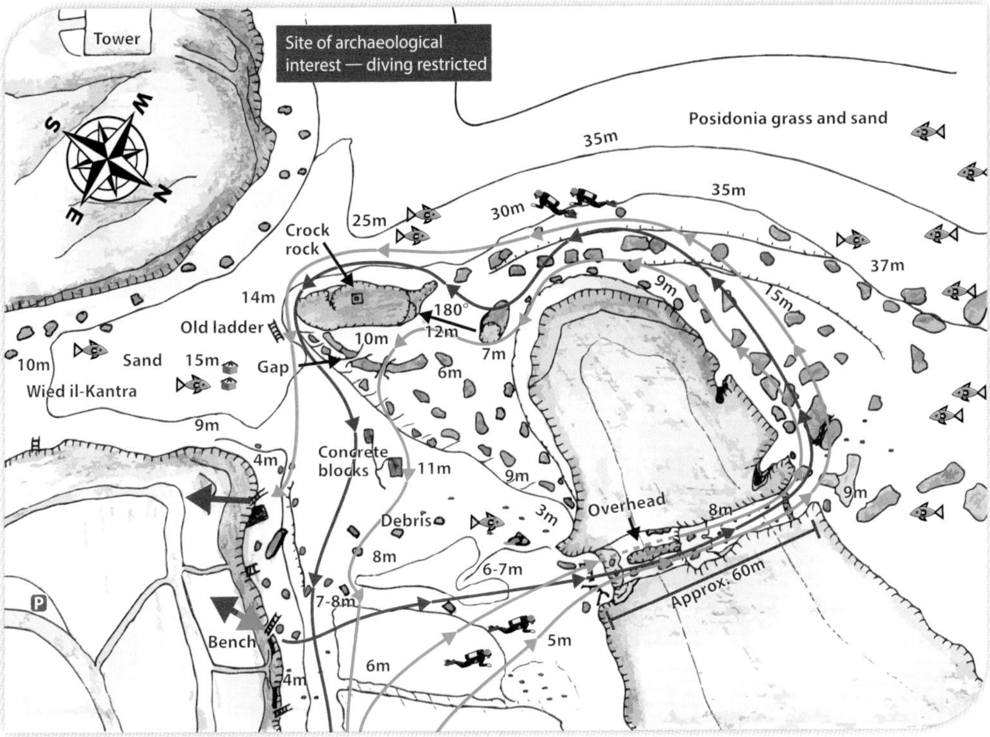

Bay and tunnel

The bay can be dived in several ways and there are many suitable entries and exits. I often enter from the white stone bench on the left side, by giant stride or by ladder. There is an additional entrance shown on the *Site 45* map. From there you can head underwater or surface swim 310° to the other side of the bay to reach the tunnel. The entrance at 4m rises to a 3m ledge just inside, it then splits around a large rock in the middle. The left-hand side is an overhead environment for about 15m. If you take the right fork look for any oncoming divers. You will notice the light diminish, but your eyes will adjust and you will be able to surface if need be. You will then see light coming from the other end. The two tunnels converge and the rocky floor drops away to pebbles at a depth of 8m. It is a further 40m to the exit.

At that point you could turn around and go back into the bay. Alternatively, turn left and follow the reef wall south for about five minutes as it turns gradually left. On your right a large rock will appear, the top of which is at 7m. Then follow the posidonia grass down to another rock at 12m on a bearing of 180° — this one has a beacon for boat traffic on it. Go around the rock (max depth 25m) until you pass an old ladder and a bank appears on your left. This leads to a 9m gap between two rocks. Go through and curve right heading about 90° over rocks to a sand and grass bottom. Or, follow the bottom of the bank from the ladder at 14m. You will find two large concrete blocks at 12m with mooring rope going up to the surface. Juvenile barracuda are often seen here in large numbers.

Head between 60° to 140° from here back into the bay, gradually getting shallower. If you keep right (south-east) you should see a bank and some ladder exits. Or you may wish to follow this bank to the end, past Churchill Restaurant, to the steps for your exit.

South-west

ROB SMITH

Xlendi tunnel

Details

Be aware of boat traffic — the use of an SMB (surface marker buoy) is recommended.
Max depth 10–20m *(33–65ft)* (if diving the tunnel)
6–10m *(20–33ft)* (in the bay)
Duration 40–60 min
★ EASY DIVE

45 XLENDI TUNNEL & REEF

Site of archaeological interest — diving restricted

80m

50m

15m

50m

60m

50m

Tower (1658)

Sand/posidonia grass

40m

45m

20m

25m

30m

25m

15m

15m

8m

Il-Kantra

25m

14m

15m

8m

6m

Sand

9m

8m

7m

P

6m

5m

3m

Statue of St Andrew

Built by the Knights of St John

From the tunnel out to the reef

On exiting the tunnel continue on a bearing of 260° over the rocks, gradually getting deeper. Go down the bank for about 80m for seven or eight minutes until you reach a large rock at 25m that overhangs onto sand. From here the bottom slopes away to posidonia grass and patchy sand and depths of 30–45m. Continue north-west for about ten minutes looking around the large rocks and sandy areas for grouper and large moray eels.

Next, turn up the rocky bank, right/70° for approximately ten minutes until you come to the 8m high reef wall with sandy patches at 15m. This leads to a wide plateau at about 8m. The wall gets smaller as the bottom to the right rises to meet it beneath the cliff. Continue with the reef wall on your left until you reach the tunnel entrance and re-enter Xlendi Bay.

Details

Max depth 2–35m *(6–115ft)*
Duration 30–80 min
★★ ADVANCED DIVE

Xlendi reef — the view on exiting the tunnel (reef side)

Xlendi is good as a night dive and octopus are often seen here

LUZZU

Traditional fishing boats are still widely used around Gozo and Malta. A luzzu (pronounced lwtsew) has a pointed double-ended hull and is brightly painted in blue, yellow, red, and green. It is a sturdy and stable boat even in bad weather. Originally equipped with sails, almost all are now motorised with small diesel engines. Some luzzu have been converted to carry tourists and some are used by dive boat operators, although the majority continue to be employed as fishing vessels.

The kajjik (pronounced kayyik) is similar but has a transom stern. Both vessels have a pair of eyes at the bow. This ancient Phoenician custom is a symbol of protection and good health, believed to protect fishermen from harm and was also followed in Greece and Egypt.

The dghajsa (pronounced die-sa) also dates back to the Phoenician era and is a traditional water taxi, which you will find on Vittoriosa Waterfront in Malta.

Eye of Horus (or of Osiris)

46 ULYSSES CAVE

Ulysses Cave sits just west of Xlendi Bay and starts inside a large cavern cut out of the cliffs that jut out over the water's edge. From a sandy 8m start, swim across a boulder slope with a narrow gully leading to a small cave at 3m. Two divers can enter and surface within it. Inside you will find beautiful green algae, purple crustose algae, and golden zoanthids. Explore the boulder field outside before eventually returning to your boat.

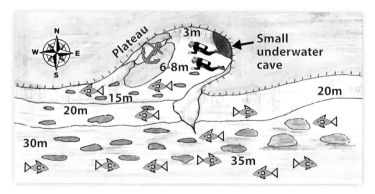

South-west

Details
Can be dived at night.
Max depth 3–30m *(10–100ft)*
Duration 30–40 min
★ EASY DIVE

Another fantastic boat dive, just a few minutes from Xlendi Bay and midway between Wardija Point and Ulysses Cave. This place is best dived in the afternoon, when the sun is high. Dive boats anchor on a plateau of rock in just 6m of water. Looking at the wall above water you will notice a shallow cavern to the west. When conditions are right, there is the opportunity for an interesting snorkel along the edge of the plateau and the vertical wall at depths of 5–10m. This area is rarely fished and shoals of bream, amberjacks, parrotfish, wrasse, damselfish and sand smelt to name but a few can be found in large numbers.

Dive

Descending onto the plateau, make your way north to the base of the wall at 8m. There you will find a gully — turn east into it, with one diver behind the other. Follow it around and under a small arch after which it turns sharply to your right. At the end of the gully, turn sharp left and over the wall with a large rock in front of you, follow the reef down to the bottom at 18m.

On your right will be a swim-through under the huge boulder that leans against the reef wall you just went over. Go through this tunnel and look on the walls and small tufts of growth for nudibranch and other forms of marine life. Exiting leads you down a slope at the base of the plateau, which goes steadily from 18m to the bottom at 50m where there will be a large pinnacle of rock above you. Follow it around to the right, then gradually ascend back up to 20–25m where there will be boulders and grassy areas all around you. Looking across to your right the plateau will never be very far from sight. As you swim over the many rocks to the reef wall you can usually spot lobsters, groupers, bream and even on occasion barracuda. As an alternative, you can follow the top of the reef shallower, at between 12–18m.

South-west

109

Eventually you will end up at the small cavern on the western/left side of the plateau. At the bottom of the back of it, there is a very small swim-through, only big enough for one diver at a time. The walls here have less growth, but on close inspection are teeming with life.

On exiting make your way to the plateau and yet another arch, at 9m. Before you get to it look around the sea floor at 16–18m. You will often see octopus, various species of anemones, sea urchins and also under the large rocks look for common spiny lobster (*Palinurus elephas*) antennas sticking out. Swimming up through the arch at 10m brings you back into the gully on top of the plateau for your safety stop. As you go through the arch look carefully for nudibranchs.

Cavern

Swimming nudibranch in the tunnel under the huge boulder

Details
Max depth 6–50m *(20–165ft)*
Duration 35–60 min
★ EASY DIVE

West

In this area

48 WARDIJA POINT (Il-Ponta tal-Wardija)

The most south-westerly dive site on Gozo, with high cliffs above it, is Wardija Point. There are not as many fish here as in other locations but diving deep down the near-vertical wall and under-hanging shelves is an amazing experience. The wall is covered in algae that has been eroded over time, creating thousands of small holes and fissures. These are now inhabited by a wide variety of marine life including the Mediterranean lobster. The bottom slopes away with boulders littering it and some huge grouper hide amongst them. Do your safety stop on the shallower areas of the wall before you return to the waiting dive boat.

Dusky grouper (Epinephelus marginatus)

Details

Conditions: This location is rather exposed, strong currents to be expected from the west at times. Check this on entry.
Max depth 20–50m *(65–165ft)*
Duration 30–50 min
Visibility normally 30m+
★★ ADVANCED DIVE

PUNIC TEMPLE (Ras il-Wardija)

The Phoenicians (or Carthaginians as they are better known) established many colonies in Malta and Gozo circa 500 BC and remained active around the islands until about 218 BC. At Ras il-Wardija there are the remains of a rock-cut sanctuary/temple site on the outskirts of Santa Lucija village. The area has amazing views of Fungus Rock *(see Site 49)* in Dwejra to the west and Xlendi *(Site 44)* a little further to the south. The site consists of a man-made cavern with niches, cisterns, troughs and a round pot-shaped well.

Gozo became a municipium after the Romans took over in 218 BC. This made it independent of Malta with a republican government and it minted its own gold coins. At about this time it is thought the temple went out of use.

Behind the temple is a hillock that may have been used as a lookout and signalling point. The temple and hillock can be reached by walking from Santa Lucija and Dwejra, or by climbing the cliffs from Xlendi Bay, making your way to a small pond containing terrapins and then following the coastal path west.

West

49 FUNGUS ROCK (Il-Gebla tal-General)

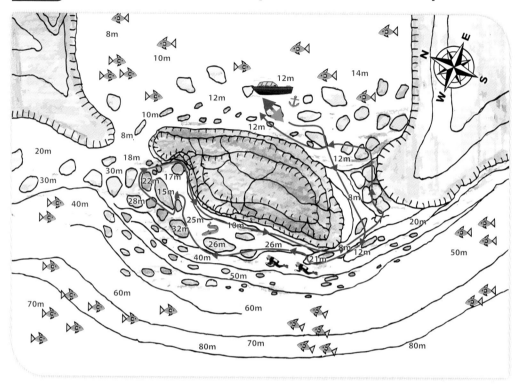

Location and History

Fungus Rock is an isolated and prominent feature in Dwejra which towers about 60m above sea level. The locals call it Il-Gebla tal-General, which means General's Rock. Legend has it that centuries ago an Italian general fell to his death here.

The name Fungus Rock is rather misleading. A plant called Maltese fungus (*Cynomorium coccineum*) was highly prized by the Knights of St John to treat all manner of illnesses and it still grows on the rock today. However, it is a parasitic plant rather than a fungus. Nowadays it is used to treat impotence, backache and to nourish the blood.

The Knights only allowed the nobility to use the plant and they often gifted it to foreign dignitaries. The rock was heavily guarded and in 1744 the Grand Master had the sides scraped smooth to make it harder for any thief to climb. Those caught trying would either be sent to their deaths or to row in the Knights' galleys for life. The Knights erected a type of man-carrying cable car system between the island and the mainland so that the plant could be collected.

In 1987 David Attenborough was granted special permission to film on the rock for the BBC production *The First Eden*.

Dive

The underwater scenery here is as dramatic as above with vertical walls to depths of 60m. There are large boulders — some sitting one on top of the other — which provide an excellent habitat for large groupers.

Starting from the sheltered left/south side of Dwejra Bay at 10–12m, follow the rock around to the right, rising to a 7m plateau. As you reach the outside reef wall the ledge drops down to 12–14m, and a hole in the shelf made by a falling boulder. Then follow along the sheer cliff wall with its ledges and small rocks, choosing your depth as it drops down to 45–55m.

Next, ascend up the bank that rises from the depths, as the wall starts to turn again to the right. Here the underwater features become more interesting as ledges, gullies and boulders present themselves, calling for closer inspection. Marine life is not as abundant here as one might expect. However, the vertical wall is covered in the usual sea urchins, tube worms, starfish and bristle worms and you will see the odd Mediterranean lobster which has found a home in one of the many holes.

On reaching the north-western corner of the rock wall (after 15–20 min) it curves around to your right leading you back.

With the reef now on your left, it is time to begin a slow ascent as you commence the journey back to the boat. Staying at about 10m follow the reef back into the bay to your pick-up point. If time and air allow, look around the bay and on the inside/eastern walls of Fungus Rock as the marine life there is abundant.

Details
Max depth 7–50m *(23–165ft)*
Duration 30–60 min
★ EASY DIVE

50 CROCODILE ROCK

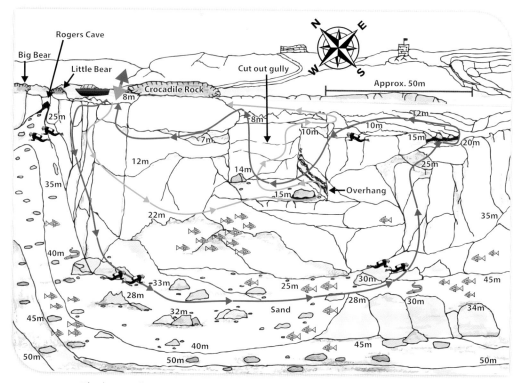

The boat will usually moor at the reef edge on the western side at about 6-8m. There is sometimes a mild current in a north-westerly or south-easterly direction, which hits the wall and speeds up over the shallower reef edge. With that in mind the boat skipper may use a swim line. Have a look at the map for *Site 51* too, as it shows some of this site from above.

On descent, head west-north-west to the edge of the reef that drops off sharply to 40–45m below you. Turn left and follow the reef down to your desired depth. By this point you should notice that the current (if any) has (usually) disappeared.

The reef wall itself is very colourful and packed full of all forms of marine life. This includes amberjack and bonito, which make quick appearances on occasions, hunting for food up and down the walls. At the bottom numerous large and small rocks are scattered around and sandy patches taper off into the distance. Large dusky grouper (*Epinephelus marginatus*), dentex (*Dentex dentex*) and Mediterranean lobster (*Panulirus elephas*) can be found here along with the smaller molluscs such as the nudibranch *Peltodoris atromaculata*. Within the walls and floor of this offshore reef you can see Mediterranean moray eel (*Muraena Helena*) and common octopus (*Octopus vulgaris*).

Looking to your left at the reef wall notice a large gully — a 20m square cut-out from the reef wall — this is rather unusual and looks in some way man-made. In the distance 30–40m away you will see much larger boulders start to emerge, but time and depth are usually up now so start your ascent by going into the cut-out gully or following the top of the reef wall at about 12m. Around the top of the reef there are usually large shoals of barracuda (*Sphyraena sphyraena*). Alternatively if air permits carry on along the wall a little further to another smaller gully some 50m away.

Making your way to the top of the gully at a depth of 8m, turn left/north-west with Crocodile Rock protruding from the water on your left. After 3–4 minutes you will reach your boat. If you have time explore the top of the reef, looking for the many forms of life that inhabit it, before ascending.

ANDREAS & CHANTEL CHIOCCHETTI

Descending into the cut-out gulley

Details

Current is sometimes strong from the north-west.
Good for novice and experienced, always a pleasurable dive.
Max depth 6–50m *(20–165ft)*
Duration 30–60 min
Visibility 20–50m
★ EASY DIVE ★★ ADVANCED DIVE

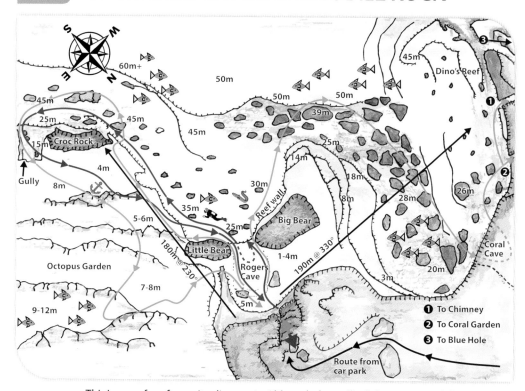

This is one of my favourite dive spots. Although the walk of about 80m with heavy equipment to and from the entry/exit may challenge some people, it is worth it. Sturdy diving rock boots are useful as the ground here is unforgiving. See also *Site 50* map.

Red Route

Enter between Little Bear and Big Bear islets, descending in 5m of water. Swim out to the edge of the reef and Rogers Cave will be below you at about 20–25m. A torch is useful but not a necessity. This cavern extends inwards 15m at a slight incline and is about 10m wide. Inside you will see lots of colourful false coral, sea potato and sponges. On exiting turn left, following the reef and eventually going around Crocodile Rock (Croc Rock). When you see the 20m wide gully make your way up it to 8m. Then turn left, keeping Croc Rock on your left and after 3–4 minutes you will reach the top of the reef again. Make your way back up the reef, north, to the exit between Little Bear and Big Bear.

Green Route

Surface swim to Croc Rock looking down at the edge of the reef on the way, so conserving your air. The reef drops off sharply to 40–45m. If you have spare time and air at the end take a look at Octopus Garden, it has lots to offer. Depending on your depth profile, this dive will take about 30–45 minutes.

Blue Route

Entering between Little Bear and Big Bear go over the reef down to Rogers Cave. From there, bear right to the reef point where it drops off dramatically to 50m on sand. Then cut across north to the Coral Cave entrance — it has a large pointed rock on its right-hand

West

side. Alternatively, keep the reef on your right and follow the bowl around. Then exit from either the Coral Garden (via **2**), Blue Hole (**3**), or use (**1**) and go down the Chimney *(see Site 53)*. You need at least 100 bar and should go no deeper than 15m as this will take you a further 6–10 minutes or so.

Left to right: The islets Crocodile Rock, Little Bear and Big Bear

Dotted sea slug/nudibranch (Peltodoris atromaculata) are common here

Details

There is sometimes a slight current from the north-west or south-east at Croc Rock, flowing over the top of the reef — take this into consideration when planning. There may also be boats moored by Croc Rock.

Max depth 6–45m *(20–150ft)*
Duration 30–60 min
★★ ADVANCED DIVE

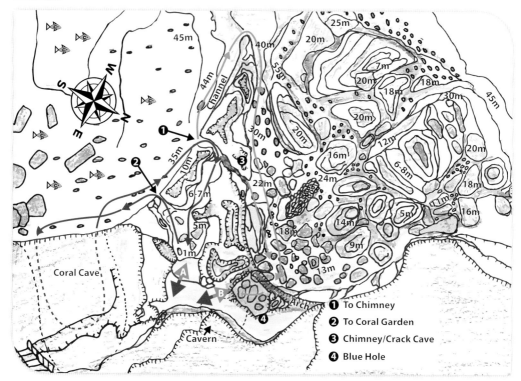

- ❶ To Chimney
- ❷ To Coral Garden
- ❸ Chimney/Crack Cave
- ❹ Blue Hole

This is a nice place to stay all day and do a combination of dives that can be achieved in different ways. Coral Cave is a large, open, overhead environment cavern and very light, even right at the back.

From the car park, walk down both sets of steps over the rocks and through the gap, turning left/south to the Coral Garden (entry A). About 15m out from the water's edge there is a ledge that drops off to 5m. Descend and keep left in this shallow area. Just one minute into the dive, on your left you will pass an interesting a hole in the reef wall — a swim-through — before reaching a vertical drop off to about 30m below, marked (**2**) on the map. Turn left here and descend to Coral Cave's large entrance which you will see after two or three minutes.

The top of this cavern is just 7m below water and at its base it is 26m. I tend to enter at the furthest point. It goes back about 60m and is filled with all sorts of life including golden cup corals, tunicates, sea sponges, tube worms, fans and anemones. Unfortunately, I have seen a decline in the health of these species and the cave's appearance over the years. This fragile community will undoubtedly be harmed by your bubbles and equipment, so **be especially careful if entering the cave** — manage your breathing by relaxing and moving slowly, watch your buoyancy and do not touch anything.

The floor rises slowly up to the back (at about 15m) and you will see some broken coral. I advise you to **leave it there** — not everyone adheres to the policy of 'look but don't touch'. Please only take memories and photographs. Please **do not enter** the large dark hole as tragically in 1999 two divers lost their lives there. It tapers to nothing and silts up very easily.

Return the same way you arrived, spending some time in Coral Garden on your way; it has an array of species including octopus, moray eels and many types of nudibranch, but as they are very small you will have to look very closely to see them.

West

Keep to the right of the wall and exit in the shallows. I prefer to inflate my jacket and surface swim face down so as not to crush the snakelock anemones (*Anemonia viridis*). Alternatively, if air permits, use entrance (**1**) and go down the Chimney (**3**) *(see Site 53)* which will take a further 6-10 minutes. You could then exit at the Blue Hole.

Looking down on the Blue Hole (right/bottom) and Coral Garden (left/top)

Spiral tube worm (Sabella spallanzanii) open and retracting into its tube

Details

Take special care in Coral Cave — see the advice above. The use of diving boots to access the site is advisable, take your time walking over the uneven surfaces of the rocks. At the car park during the summer a shower is situated between the toilets.

Max depth 6–30m *(20–100ft)*

Duration 35–55 min

★ EASY DIVE

★★ ADVANCED DIVE

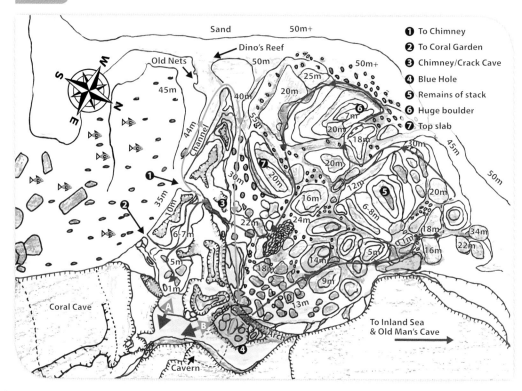

West

Location and access

The Blue Hole is probably the most popular dive site on Gozo. This was also the location of the Azure Window — the much loved, iconic, beautiful, natural stone arch. It sadly fell into the sea during a storm in March 2017, the inevitable victim of the natural forces which have sculpted the coastline over the ages. It featured in many films, such as *Odyssey* (1997), *Clash of the Titans* (1981) and *The Count of Monte Cristo* (2002) and the first television series of *Game of Thrones* (2011). When I guide here I usually walk up to the ridge of rock overlooking the area, as this gives everyone a sense of perspective and it is a nice spot for a photograph. The walk to the water can be quite a trek from the car park and then slippery right up to the edge of the hole. You can sit there to put your fins on, or do it in the water. Be aware of other divers completing safety stops below you.

Dive

The collapse of the Azure Window, although extremely sad, has opened up some new opportunities for divers. This is still an outstanding dive site and many things remain the same. The column which once supported the arch fell mostly to the south and east, creating a new shallow playground for novices. Going deeper, you will find the largest parts between the 12m shelf and the Chimney — three huge boulders, one of which rises from the depths all the way up to 7m (**6**). There are new swim-throughs. The old top slab is 10–15m away from the Chimney, lying on its side (**7**). Debris litters the sea floor. The new top of the stack is now underwater, almost breaking the surface (**5**).

   Starting in the Blue Hole (**B**), the rocky bottom will be 13–17m below. Go under the 10m wide arch, the top of which is covered in golden cup corals, at just 7m. Head north-west and complete a tour of the boulders which formed the Azure Window (including **5**, **6** and **7**). The views from the north-western side are as spectacular as ever and full of life, so remember to stop and look back. If you want to there are swim-throughs at around 20m (north of **5**) and 23m (beside **6**). Then head south-east to the entrance at 16m to the reef and Chimney (**3**) (sometimes called Crack Cave). First, look to see if a diver is coming down and ask how many there are behind them — you may need to change your plan. Leave space between you and the diver in front. The Chimney is about 15m long, with the top at 7m. Be mindful of the buoyancy change as you ascend it. That will take about 30 minutes. At this point you have three options depending on air consumption:

1. A diver with 80 bar or less can turn left at the top of the Chimney, go into Coral Garden and use (A). This is the nearest exit available and is the red route.
2. With 90–110 bar, you can go over the top of the Chimney, through the bubbles rising from it, turn right, follow the wall along for 50m and exit at the Blue Hole (B).
3. With 110 bar or more you can turn right at (**1**) and follow the edge of the reef, turning right again, past the Chimney to the Blue Hole. This route may produce sightings of amberjacks and barracuda. This ending is shown as the green route.

At the back of the Blue Hole you will see a large cave about 25m in diameter and about 10m high. It is perfect for photography (but note that this is an overhead environment).

This dive is just as nice the other way around, start in Coral Garden (A) and follow the red route in reverse — useful if the Blue Hole is busy on arrival.

Details

When ascending in the Blue Hole be aware of others descending above you. Visibility is usually very good here except after rain.

Max depth 6–50m *(20–165ft)*

Duration 30–60 min

★ EASY DIVE (following the course at max 18m) ★★ ADVANCED DIVE

Divers at entry B, the Blue Hole — the Azure Window used to stand in the background

OCEANFOTO.CO.UK

The Azure Window before it collapsed

OCEANFOTO.CO.UK

Conger eel at the back of the Blue Hole cavern

JACEK MADEJSKI

Entering the Blue Hole cavern

OCEANFOTO.CO.UK

The column now almost breaks the surface (5 on the map on page 122)

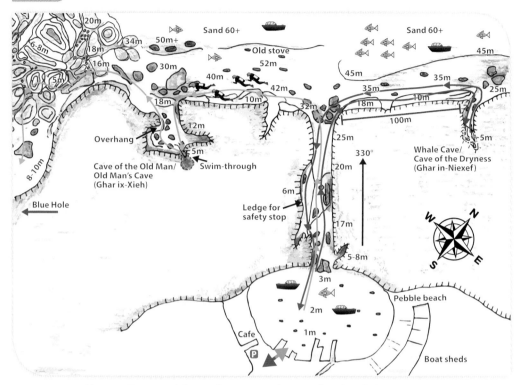

Also see *Site 55* and *Site 56* for maps with more detail and alternative angles plus some additional photos. The Inland Sea is an area of shallow water with an open tunnel leading to the ocean. Boat trips can take you to see the cliffs, Tal-Barba *(see Site 56)* and Old Man's Cave. By the beach there is a café that serves drinks and homemade cake. It is in a converted boathouse with seating outside under a canopy. A portaloo toilet is installed here in summer.

Dive

Be aware of any boat traffic and keep to the left-hand side near the tunnel entrance. When entering or leaving the tunnel — whether you are above or below water — look and listen for boats. Other divers may be coming out or doing safety stops. Carry on down the slope — it gets gradually darker as you swim, with the light behind you. At this point a torch may be useful. However, your eyes will adjust to the natural light coming from the other end in the form of a long shaft of blue. It is an impressive sight — two vast columns of rock on either side of you.

Once all the way through, turn left and follow the reef wall for ten minutes. Set your depth, at this point I rarely go beyond 20–25m. The seabed starts to fall away to 50m but conserve your air and avoid the temptation to go deep. Look into the blue for hunting barracuda and amberjacks. Eventually, you will come to Old Man's Cave. A ledge of rock leads to the large floor inside at 12m and on to a small chamber at 5m. You can swim-through the top opening and exit through the bottom one, at 8m.

Turn left out of the cavern, going under a rock at 12m which juts out from the reef wall. Continue with the wall on your left. After about ten minutes you will come to the resting place of the Azure Window, which collapsed in March 2017 *(see Site 53)*. Boulders of all sizes now litter the seabed, and the bottom of the column is just below the surface. Carry on swimming for a further 25m to the Blue Hole arch and exit there.

JACEK MADEJSKI

Exiting the Old Man's Cave swim-through

Details

If you plan to exit at the Blue Hole it's best to leave your vehicle in the car park nearest to it. Consider current and swell — you don't want to be making this journey if the current is against you.

Max depth 10–50m *(33–165ft)*

Duration 40–55 min

★ EASY DIVE ★★ ADVANCED DIVE

CATHERINE & JEAN-PIERRE CORNAND

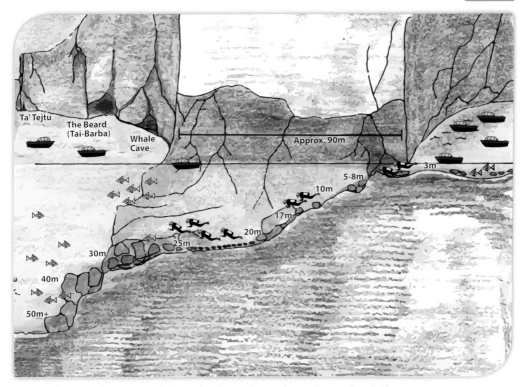

Ta' Tejtu

The Beard
(Tai-Barba)

Whale
Cave

Approx. 90m

3m

5-8m

10m

17m

20m

25m

30m

40m

50m+

West

Also see the maps for *Site 54* and *Site 56* for alternative angles and more detail. The entrance and tunnel part of this dive is identical to *Site 54*, so read the advice there too. As before, be aware of boat traffic — it can get busy in the summer months. Swim out on the left-hand side before descending near the tunnel entrance at 3m, looking and listening for boat traffic and other divers coming out or doing a safety stop. Inside, keep an eye out for dusky groupers — they often lie on the rocks at 7m. Carry on down into the tunnel and the bottom will start to slope gradually, you will see boulders and it will get darker as you leave the light behind you. A torch may be useful at this point but it is not essential.

At the seaward exit, with your depth about 26m, turn right and follow the reef wall. Look for John dory (*Zeus Faber*, which means 'blacksmith of the gods'). Set your maximum depth depending on your qualification and experience, but I rarely go beyond 20–25m as it is about a 90m swim to Whale Cave. Following the reef wall around until it turns sharply to the right, this will take approximately 16–22 minutes.

Whale Cave is not an overhead environment, so you can surface if you need to. Small tourist boats may motor into this cavern. The underwater entrance at 25m is pebbly and about 14m wide. As you go in look out for little nudibranch and flatworms on the smaller rocks. Looking ahead and slightly right you will see a large rock that you can swim underneath. Follow the rocks up and up from 22m to 6m at the back, then turn around to reveal the cavern's sizeable walls and look down at where you have just come from.

Start your return journey shallow, keeping left. Sometimes, small bubbles which were trapped when you went under the rock 15m below will be rising up. From this point you should have a minimum of 100 bar left in your tank. Make your way back along the reef wall and into the Inland Sea tunnel. Keep over to the right side, looking for the ledge at 6m for several reasons: it is at the perfect depth for a safety stop; you can keep out of the

way of boat traffic; it has good views and there is some life in the cracks and crevices.
When you are ready make your way out, listening for boat traffic.

ROB SMITH

John dory (Zeus faber)

Details
Watch your depth and air consumption.
Max depth 6–50m *(20–165ft)*
Duration 45–55 min
★ EASY DIVE ★★ ADVANCED DIVE

West

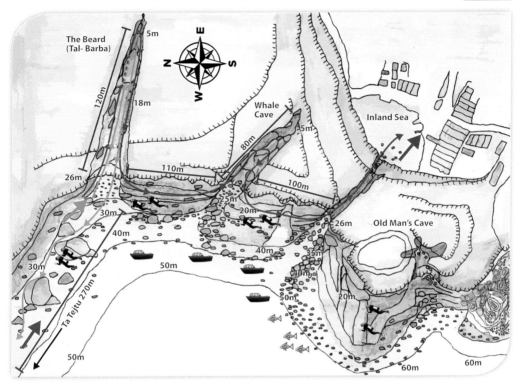

Tal-Barba (The Uncle or Beard) is a very pleasant dive. It is a cavern about 200m to the north of the Inland Sea. Tal Barba is so called as the entrance is much wider at the bottom than at the top, making it resemble a man's beard.

Your boat may drop you outside the cave and pick you up further round the reef — turn right on exiting (blue route). Or you may turn left and exit on the shore at the Inland Sea (red route). Whatever your arrangement is, you will not regret or forget this great dive.

I find the colours of the marine life at the entrance and the walls on either side quite startling and very healthy. Crustose algae (*Pseudolithophyllum expansum*), golden cup corals (*Astroides calycularis*), red sea stars (*Echinaster sepositus*), red sea squirt (*Halocinthya papillosa*) and false corals (*Myriapora truncate*) amongst many others adorn the cave and rocks. As you get deeper into the The Beard these gradually become sparser, leaving just bare limestone.

Make your way slowly to the back, gently rising up past small rocks to a boulder above you that is wedged-in about half way down the shaft. Continue in with the light fading and the walls narrowing to the top. There is a flat narrow ledge and a halocline often appears at about 8m from the fresh water seeping through from above. It is possible to surface here.

Next, turn around and go over the wedged rock that you went under earlier. Swim out shallower for about 90m in single file. Looking ahead the shaft of light will start to get larger and the beard shape appears as the opening gets wider.

On exiting you have the option of turning left or right depending on how you plan to finish the dive. If turning right follow the reef wall around where you will see large rocks strewn about, gradually falling away to greater depths. The visibility here is usually very good. Eventually do a safety stop against the wall and exit to the waiting boat.

Alternatively, turning left leads you to Whale Cave and all it has to offer *(see Site 55)*. Finally make your way back to the Inland Sea entrance and stay over to the right-hand side. Look for the ledge at 6m, do your safety stop there away from any boats and then make your way out, listening for marine traffic.

The Beard

Whale Cave

Red scorpionfish (Scorpaena scrofa)

Details
Max depth 28m *(90ft)* (40–50m *(130–165ft)* if doing the reef)
Duration 45–55 min
★★ ADVANCED DIVE

West

The sharp lines of the cliffs above water extend below the surface to the rocky seabed, and there is a gradual slope on the southern side. This site is best dived in the afternoon as the sun shines directly onto the reef wall illuminating the dive quite spectacularly. The visibility is usually very good here. The boat will not usually anchor. However, weather-permitting it may do so on the 10–15m plateau that extends from the cliff on the south-western side of the first cavern, which is a square cut tunnel that can be seen above water.

Dive

Descend and go through the tunnel at 5–6m. It leads to a drop-off with a rather nice chute and a vertical wall on your right. Some 40m further on there is a cavern at 20m, with a sandy floor.

To your left, large boulders litter the seabed all around you at 30–45m. Marine life has never been spectacular here but on closer inspection you will find many interesting things around the rocks and sandy floor. One such is the sea potato, a heart-shaped sea urchin. Their white, spineless, brittle skeletons are sometimes found on beaches. Live sea potatoes are covered in spines which lie flat across their bodies. The spines are a lot shorter than other sea urchins and look more like hair — giving them the overall appearance of a hairy potato. They eat organic waste and this makes them highly sensitive to pollution on the sea floor. Other forms of marine life I have found here include Mediterranean moray, small lobsters, lots of cardinalfish and shoals of cow bream (*Sarpa salpa*).

Make your way back/south, through the tunnel or up the slope to the right of the arch and onto the plateau to your waiting boat, doing your safety stop on the way.

Details

Some large boulders are in deep water, making this a rather short no decompression adventure. Be aware of time and depth.
Max depth 10–40m *(30–130ft)*
Duration 40–60 min
★ EASY DIVE

Comino Island

In this area

A SHORT HISTORY

Comino is named after the cumin plant, the seed having been harvested in Roman times where it was used in the same way as pepper is today. Like most spices, cumin was also valued for its health and medicinal benefits.

Comino is peaceful and quiet. The stars in the night sky seem to be bigger and brighter here as there is less light pollution. It has been uninhabited for most of its history but has often been used as a place of imprisonment or exile. During the Roman period and in the Middle Ages pirates hid in its caves and caverns and used the jagged coastline to prey on passing boats. The topography below the waves mirrors that above with the many tunnels and arches making it a diver's playground.

King Alphonse V of Aragon was petitioned by local people in 1416 to build a tower for protection on Comino and monies were raised by putting a tax on imported wine. However, the tower did not materialise. Eventually, two hundred years later (in 1618) the Knights of St John erected St Mary's Tower (it-Torri ta' Santa Marija) using money collected from the sale of brushwood. It was part of a chain of defensive towers built across the Maltese islands. St Mary's Tower doubled as the Chateau d'If in Kevin Reynolds 2002 film, *The Count of Monte Cristo*. Following restoration in 2002, it is now open to the public (when the flag is flying above it).

The Knights hunted on Comino and were highly protective of the local game and seasonal birds. If caught poachers were sentenced to up to three years as a slave on one of their galleys.

In the past whenever the seas were too rough for the Gozitan priest to make the crossing to Comino for the celebration of Holy Mass, the local community would gather on the rocks at Dahlet il-Ħmara across the channel and look towards the Chapel il-Madonna tal-Blat (Saint Mary of the Rocks), in Hondoq, Gozo, where Mass was being conducted. They followed along with the progression of the service by means of a complex flag code.

Blue Lagoon
Between Comino and the islet of Cominotto are the crystal clear waters of the Blue Lagoon. This area is frequented by many boats and tourists during the summer months, when a swimming area is created between the islands which boats are prohibited from entering.

GETTING THERE

Comino lies between Gozo and the main island of Malta. It measures 2.68km (1.66 miles) long by 2.19km (1.36 miles) wide. It is part of the municipality of Għajnsielem, in Gozo.

Unless on a dive boat, to access Comino you will need to use one of the many ferry boats. The trip takes about 15 minutes and it is also possible to visit the Comino Caves. You can buy hot and cold food and beverages in the Blue Lagoon.

- **Ebsons Comino Ferries:** Provides a round trip service from Mġarr Harbour, Gozo and from Ċirkewwa, Malta (near the ferry) or Marfa (near Riviera Hotel) to Comino Island / Blue Lagoon. Boats leave every hour on a daily basis during the summer months.
  Website: www.cominoferryservice.com
- **The Comino Hotel:** Also offers this service between April and October when the hotel is open.
  Tel: +356 21529821.
  Email: info@cominohotel.com
  Website: www.cominohotel.com
- **Captain Morgan Cruises:**
  Tel: + 356 2346 3333.
  Email info@captainmorgan.com.mt
  Website: www.captainmorgan.com.mt
- **Joyride Water Sports:** based in Hondoq Bay. Boat trips around Gozo and Comino.
  Tel: +356 9924 9251.
  Website: www.joyridewatersports.com
- **United Comino Ferries:**
  Tel: +356 9940 6529.
  Website: www.cominoferries.com

Comino Island

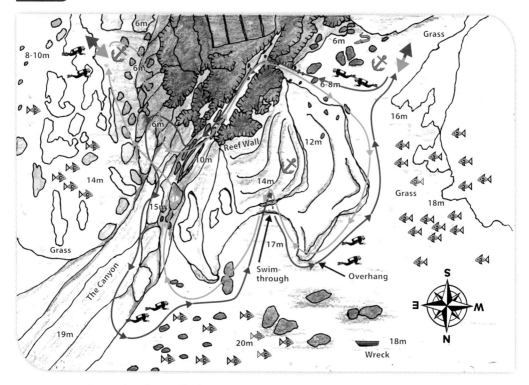

Situated in the north of Comino on the western side of San Niklaw Bay, this site features drop-offs, an arch, a canyon, other rock formations including a swim-through and the remains of a traditional fishing boat. The seabed here is a combination of sand, rock and posidonia grass. The canyon itself has been crafted over thousands of years by the action of the sea and extends for over 300m.

Dive

Depending on wind direction, your boat will anchor on either the south-east or south-west shelf in 6–8m of water. If you descend from the south-west, head south-east through an arch at 6m. This was used in the film *Clash of the Titans* (1981), it is where Poseidon (Jack Gwillim) releases The Kraken. Next, turn left into the start of the canyon and swim north-wards to a maximum depth of about 19m, where there will be rocks, grass and patches of sand on either side.

Cross over the left-hand side of the canyon and head back in a southerly direction until at about 17m you hit the edge of a semi-circular wall. You will see a swim-through and slightly to your right at the end, a small overhang. Do the swim-through up to the next level at 14m. Then carry on along the wall right/north to the end and the overhang. North of this position you will find the remains of the old fishing boat.

Next, turn south and follow the reef wall back to your waiting boat.

There are also some nice overhangs and a couple of small caverns along the wall on the south-eastern side. Take your time and explore these well if you start that side, or as a slight detour from the canyon. Moray eels, banded sea bream and the occasional barracuda are just a few of the fish that frequent this site. Seeing an octopus or small shrimps in the caves and under rocks is not uncommon.

Two-banded sea bream (Diplodus vulgaris)

Details

This site is unfortunately a little forgotten and is rarely dived, but is excellent and is suitable for all levels.

Max depth 2–20m *(6–65ft)*

Duration 30–60 min

★ EASY DIVE

59 SANTA MARIJA REEF

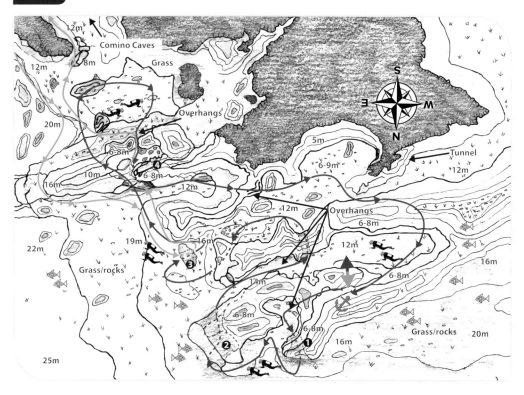

This dive truly is a playground for divers — it is not too deep so it affords you plenty of time to explore and see what you can find. Your boat will anchor in 9m of water on a rock plateau about 35m from land.

Dive

Descend and follow the plateau down into a stony circular gully at 13m. This steps down, heading northwards to an overhanging tunnel (**1**) and then drops further to 18m on the other side. Follow the 4m high wall around in a south-easterly direction to the end of the reef where there is another overhanging tunnel at about 17m (**2**).

It leads out to a large free-standing boulder that has two small holes to swim through (**3**), each about 2m long. To the south-east the reef flows around and over to a small cavern before going around the corner. About 10m away there is a hole at 14m, go through and up to 8–9m. In front of you is an overhang that looks like a shark's head with its mouth open (**4**). Above this at 6–7m is the fin — which seems to be pointing in the wrong direction.

Turning to your right/north-west, make your way over the higher part of this reef at 9–12m and back to your waiting boat. There is still plenty of opportunity to explore around the shallow waters to the south if you wish, air permitting.

OCEANFOTO.CO.UK

OCEANFOTO.CO.UK

Comino Island

Details
Max depth 2–22m *(6–70ft)*
Duration 30–60 min
★ EASY DIVE

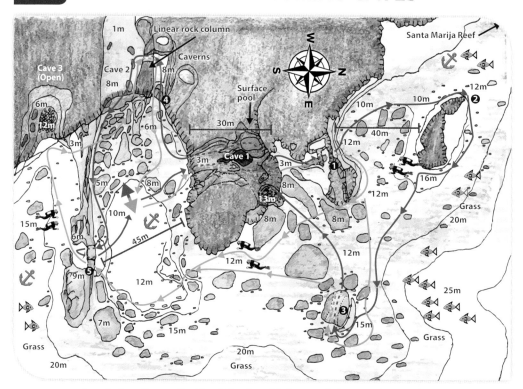

Located on the north side of Comino, this is one of the most interesting cave systems in the world. The picturesque caves and surrounding area featured in the film *The Count of Monte Cristo* (2002). A torch is useful but not a necessity whereas a camera is essential. This is an easy dive with access to the surface most of the time and some breathtaking views into the blue through the tunnel entrances and exits. Sun-rays create dramatic shafts of light which protrude through openings, making for a wonderful experience.

Dive

This is the red route, the blue and green routes show variations. On descent to the sandy bottom at 10m large numbers of white bream will wait to greet divers and snorkellers. Head to Cave 1 — you should see it clearly from where your boat moors. Look for the nudibranch *Cratena peregrine*, which is endemic to the Mediterranean, on the entrance walls at 3.5m. Keep right through the 15m tunnel to a small opening (for one diver) leading to a chamber with a large domed overhang. Light protrudes through holes creating 'God's Fingers'. Keep left until you get to shallow open pits in the rocky floor and you see two shards of rock nearly meeting horizontally at 4m (**1**). To your right a large rock sits on three small stumps, creating multiple options to swim-through. Go through and continue down the bank turning right to 14–18m (**2**), circling back to the cavern crossing large rocks and a small swim-through at 15m (**3**).

Turn south-west and head back into the cavern at 6m. Look for the shallow pool at 2m where it is possible to surface. Continue down the tunnel ahead and on exit turn west towards Cave 2, 10m away over *Posidonia oceanica* (sea grass) and boulders.

Enter the cavern (to the right of Cave 2) (**4**). Notice a hole above you (at 6m) and a dead-end cavern to your right with a sandy bottom (at 8m). In front, on your left, there are two tight one-person swim-throughs. The first is a circular hole through the rock, the second

Comino Island

goes up to a chamber with a sharp left turn. All lead to Cave 2 — a white sandy overhang that gets very shallow at the back. Boat traffic enters this cave **so I never do**, instead I exit straight away. Cross over to the reef on the right following a ridge of rock to the arch 25m away (**5**), or go to Cave 3. Then head back to your boat.

CATHERINE & JEAN-PIERRE CORNAND

CLAUDINE MARTIN LE COQ

Swim-through with two shards of rock almost meeting horizontally

Details

Be aware that boats will go into the cave/cavern entrances — stay low.
Max depth 8–18m *(25–60ft)*
Duration 30–70 min
★ EASY DIVE

Comino Caves Arch

Santa Marija/Comino Caves

ELEPHANT ROCK/THE MOLAR (Id-Darsa)

On the north-eastern point of Comino there is a large rock formation which extends into the water and resembles the head of an elephant. It is known locally as Id-Darsa or The Molar. There is a 30m long cave at 6m and several smaller swim-throughs around the slopes where large boulders lie on top of each other.

Dive

The reef area slopes away reaching approximately 18–20m with boulders and small patches of sand and posidonia grass. I see no reason to go any deeper than 20m or so here as the main features are the tunnel and swim-throughs. At a depth of just 6m they provide shelter to various types of fish including groupers and octopus. Sometimes we might encounter a mild current but you can use this to drift and cover a large area during a long and relaxed dive.

This is also the perfect place for snorkellers to swim from a boat.

Details

Max depth 6–20m *(20–65ft)*
Duration 30–60 min
★ EASY DIVE

Comino Island

62 SULTAN ROCK

This is the site where *HMS Sultan* holed her hull on an uncharted rock in the Comino Channel in 1889. She was built in Chatham Dockyard and launched in 1870. She weighed 9,290 tons and was 99m long. Over the course of a week she slowly filled with water before a gale saw her slip off the rock and sink. She was refloated, repaired and continued in service. If you are lucky you might find some pieces of wreckage left behind.

The seabed in this area is strewn with some huge boulders covered with marine flora and also various species of marine animals including grouper, octopus and moray eels. About 50m from the rocky cliffs the depth is around 14m on a bank that slopes down to over 30m with a sand and Posidonia grass bottom.

White-spotted octopus (Callistoctopus macropus)

Details

Max depth 10–40m *(30–130ft)*
Duration 40–50 min
★ EASY DIVE

CHRIS HOWELL

This ship had many names after being built by Frerich Schiffswerft, Nordenham, Germany as the *FV Ostmark* in 1934. These included *Popi FV*, and *Balje*. She started her life as a trawler and was used by the *Kriegsmarine* (German navy) during World War II. She was fitted with one triple-expansion diesel engine and an exhaust turbine which gave her a top speed of 12 knots. She weighed around 470 tons, was about 51m long, 8m wide and 4m in height.

By this time a Panamanian freighter under the name *Popi FV*, she was wrecked in March 1971, possibly in bad weather, by running aground in a small cove on the southern shore of Comino. There were no casualties. She was travelling from the Grand Harbour, Malta to Tripoli, Libya. Her cargo consisted mostly of cigarettes but locals will also tell you about smuggled goods…

Dive

Large chunks of scattered wreckage lie between rocks, including parts of the stern, at a depth of roughly 10m. These mostly consist of unrecognisable twisted metal, located just a few metres south of the Wied Ernu cove jetty. Locals have memories of cigarettes floating around the area for days — it can still bring smiles to their faces when asked about this wreck.

Details

The site is easily accessed by boat, however anchorage in the area is restricted due to the presence of cables linking Comino with Malta.

Max depth 10–30m *(33–100ft)*
Duration 40–60 min
★ EASY DIVE

Comino Island

Popi FV — anchorage is restricted to due undersea cables

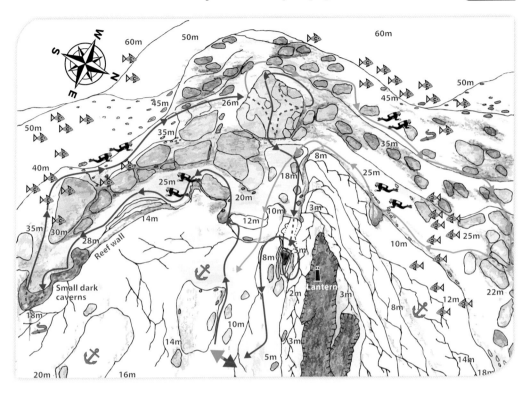

Ras L-Irqieqa (meaning narrow point) is a popular dive located on the south-eastern tip of Comino. The boat anchors between 6 and 12m on the reef opposite the old lantern. There is sometimes a westerly current flowing over the reef, and a current line may therefore be used from the boat.

On descent head west, following the reef to a ledge in the wall where to your left there is a large open crack. Follow the passage, passing large rocks as you go for a distance of about 40m. Keeping the reef on your left, carry on down to a depth of 30m and small caverns will appear in the reef wall. Turn right (do a U-turn) passing a large rock on your right. Swim for a further 40m, still at 30m in depth.

The open ocean will be on your left, with a sandy bottom at 40m gradually sloping to 50m in the dark distance. Follow the boulders on your right and you will reach a roundish boulder the size of a small house. Underneath it and above a rocky shelf at 26m, is the opening to a passage that is about 1.5m high and divers can enjoy a maze of tunnels underneath. There is usually enough natural light under here but a small torch is useful.

You will exit on the eastern or northern side of the boulder and should head east-north-east, where both walls meet and narrow. At the back at 12m is a hole (one diver at a time) that is the start of the chimney (see photo on page 150). It levels out to a sandy floor and continues along a passage with room for only one diver, although it is wide enough to manoeuvre without touching the side walls. This then opens out at an incline through a shaft at 15m which leads up to the rocky reef floor above at 5m. Your bubbles will escape from tiny openings in the rock — a wonderful sight on exiting. This chimney — along with the house-sized boulder swim-throughs — is the highlight of the site.

The red route can also be done the other way around — diving down the chimney, turning

Comino Island

right to the swim-through and back under the large round rock, turning left on exiting to the reef wall, ascending and coming back to the boat following the reef wall north-west.

Normally this dive offers incredible visibility and the chance of encounters with larger marine life. Sightings of barracuda are commonplace here along with forkbeards and lobster within the tunnels. I've even seen a *Mola mola* on two separate occasions.

Having descended the chimney this diver faces the swim-through which leads to the house-sized boulder

Lantern Point

Details
Max depth 6–50m *(20–165ft)*
Duration 40–60 min
★★ ADVANCED DIVE with depth, otherwise ★ EASY DIVE

Comino Island

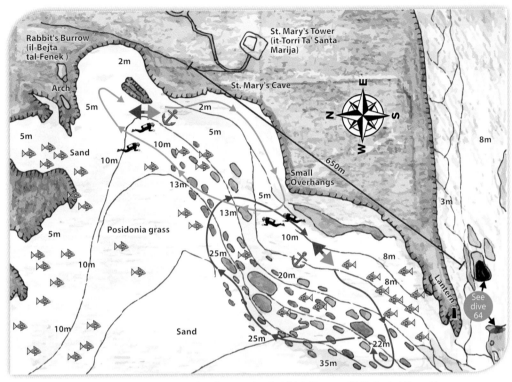

On the northern side of Lantern Point, leading to the Rabbit's Burrow (il-Bejta tal-Fenek) and on to Crystal Lagoon you will encounter a near vertical wall. At the south-western end there are large boulders interspersed with smaller rocks as it slopes down to a sandy bottom. Nearer the middle of this, beneath St Mary's Tower is a small cavern.

This reef is 650m long so you may not complete it all in one dive. You could split it into deep and shallow dives, depending on where your boat moors and circumstances.

The further north-east (and nearer to Crystal Lagoon) you go the shallower you will be, with vast meadows of *Posidonia oceanica*. There is a small cavern at 10m and many overhangs. The dive here is quite a pleasant one with a lot of marine species in shallow water found generally on the slopes and sandy bottom including shoals of bream, barracuda, octopus and flying gurnard. Rays and John dory have also been seen.

Blue route

With your boat anchoring in about 5m of water, make your way from the Rabbit's Burrow — a shallow inlet about 3m at its entrance tapering to nothing at the back (see photo on page 152) — following the reef wall in a south-westerly direction. Swim for as long as you wish to, slowly looking around and then turn north-west for a short while then finally north-east, making your way across the sand and returning to your waiting boat.

Red route

Alternatively, nearer to the lantern in 10–14m of water, head down the rocky slope southwest to the sandy bottom at 35m. Then turn north-east for a while, before heading south-east back up the slope into shallower water. Turn right at the reef wall, which should lead you back to your boat.

Comino Island

Il-Bejta tal-Fenek — The Rabbit's Burrow

Sea bream (Sarpa salpa)

Details

Be aware of boat traffic in shallow water.

Max depth 2–35m *(6–115ft)*

Duration 40–70 min

★ EASY DIVE

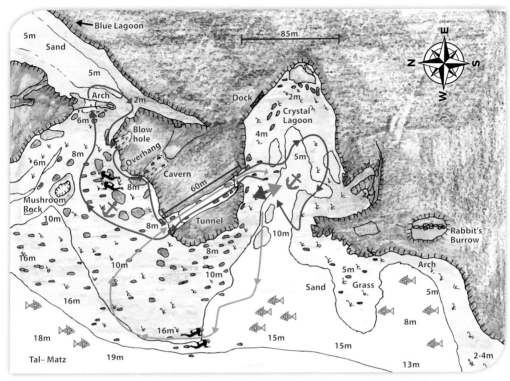

This dive is so nice that whether you are a novice or a professional there is something for everybody. It includes a 60m-long open tunnel, a great natural archway with smooth walls, a blowhole with amazing shafts of light penetrating the water and an overhang. On top of that it is also a breeding ground for octopus, flying gurnards, scorpionfish and many other varieties of marine life. You will want to investigate this spot at least once, if not more.

As this site is shallow you can look forward to a long and relaxed dive. There are plenty of white sandy areas and patches of sea grass inside the bay and with the way the light streams through from above the many unusual rock formations it is great for photographers. The tunnel is a particularly good photo opportunity as the light streams through the normally crystal clear water. As the tunnel is open on the top this is a good location for those who wish to experience diving in a slightly confined environment in complete safety. It is also good for snorkelling.

Red route

With the boat anchored inside the bay, make your way through the tunnel, turning right at the end. Head north-east towards Mushroom Rock then turn east towards the arch. Go through and turn 90° right (south) onto sand for 20m. Then catch the edge of the reef and keeping it on your left follow it around to the west, passing the blowhole and going into a strange cavern. Continue along the wall for another 20m and you will be back at the tunnel. Follow this to the end and eventually you will get back to your waiting boat inside the Crystal Lagoon. Alternatively you can follow the wall back into the bay.

Be aware that there might be boat traffic moored or moving around the lagoon so deploying a delayed SMB before surfacing may be a good idea.

Comino Island

Crystal Lagoon

Details
Max depth 2–16m *(6–50ft)*
Duration 40–80 min
★ EASY DIVE

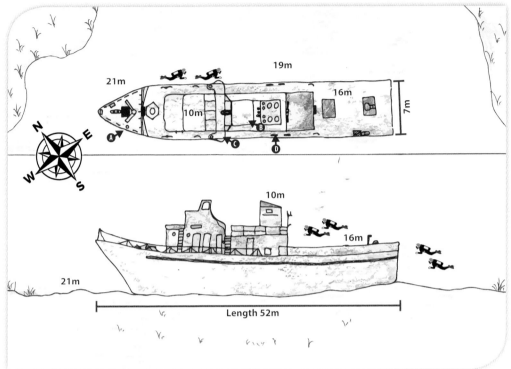

The *P31* was a Kondor Class minesweeper built at Peenewerft, Wolgast, East Germany in 1960. She was 52m long, 7m wide and weighed 360 tons. In 1992 the *P31* was given to the Armed Forces Malta (AFM). After serving 13 years she was decommissioned and sold to the Malta Tourist Authority (MTA). They scuttled her as a diving attraction in August 2009 in the middle of the bay, about halfway between Alex's Cave and Lantern Point on a sand and sea grass bottom. In the summer months there is a yellow buoy fixed just 30m away to port in an area called Tal-Matz (marked on the *Site 66* map).

This wreck sits in a maximum of 21m (at the bow), has a slight list to the port side and is very accessible. Those who have never explored inside a wreck before but who wish to do so **please seek guidance from a local professional**.

Dive

On descent from the anchor line and starting at the bow, from the seabed looking up you will see how she slightly lists to port. There is something that looks like a hexagonal seat on the bow deck — this is where the 14.5mm anti-aircraft gun would have been fixed, and in front of which is the forward hatch.

Moving along the port side, notice the abundance of marine life that has made the wreck its home in such a short time. At the stern, now partly buried by sand, the shafts are still in place but the propellers have been removed.

Moving up on to the stern deck at 16m, enter the rear hold, the first of three rectangular holes cut in the deck. Although light penetrates into the wreck there are many dark areas, so you will need a good torch. Continue forward inside toward the engine room. This still has most of its knobs and dials, although the engine itself was removed before she was sunk.

Make your way through the interior structure and exit the rear hold near the smoke

Comino Island

stack. Then swim through either the port or starboard door — both lead back inside. Move towards the bow and you can exit through the narrow bow hatch.

From the starboard door, with the toilet on your left, turn right and go past the galley. In the floor a round hatch with a ladder leads below deck to the hold which contains loose material and wires.

At the bottom of the ladder below deck, turn left to the radio room or right to the forward hatch. The radio room is about 5m away and is quite dark and confined. To your right will be two doors, take the left-hand one and then exit the wreck via the forward/bow hatch which will be just in front of you.

The wheelhouse on top at 10m has six small windows. A single door can be used for your entry and exit. Be aware of loose steel panelling and wires in here. Back on deck, the main mast has been taken away (it was originally laid across amidships).

The shallow depth and visibility usually make this a great opportunity for underwater photographers — quite often the whole wreck can be seen, from bow to stern. Marine life is rapidly populating it with bream, octopus, cuttlefish and even triggerfish having been spotted around the stern. Marine growth has also started to take hold.

Left to right: smoke stack (just visible), engine room (largest opening) and stern entry (far right)

Details
Max depth 2–15m *(5–50ft)*
Duration 30–60 min
★ EASY DIVE
★★ ADVANCED DIVE
(If going inside the wreck)

Anti-aircraft gun emplacement

ALEX'S CAVE

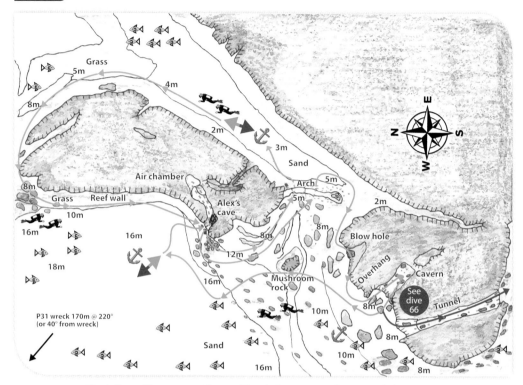

Alex's Cave, Champagne Cave or Tony's Cave as it is alternatively known, is located on one of Comino's smaller uninhabited islands on the north-west side. It measures 180m long by about 80m at its widest point.

Green route

The boat moors somewhere on the southern half of the island at a maximum depth of about 16m. Descend onto the large sandy area where you will find cleaver wrasse, cuttlefish, flounder, sea potato, flying gurnard and other interesting forms of life. Then go over to the colourful wall, which is full of life, to find the cavern entrance. Follow the wall south-east until a large opening in the reef wall appears.

Alex's Cave is about 8m wide at its sandy base, tapering to 3m at its top. The whole tunnel and is about 40m long. The ceiling stretches up to the surface, giving you a little more daylight and enticing you further inside. Follow its smoothed limestone walls — they curve left 4–5m and the light starts to disappear. As you continue your eyes will adjust to the darkness, but this part of the dive is only recommended for more experienced divers — you cannot always see the end (and the light). Also, it depends on how many divers enter. Six is comfortable but if your group is bigger it is best to stagger your entries.

At the back of the cave an oval shaft 4m across rises from 14m to the surface — it is a good place to see lots of shrimp. Any issues with equalising should be considered before ascending here, as the only exit is back the way you have just come. If you surface you will not find any treasure but a small shaft of light reflecting off the rocks above you.

Turn around and exit the way you entered. Bearing left at the entrance, follow the wall around at a depth of 6m for about 80m towards a small natural stone arch. Turn right after going under the arch, passing along a sandy patch for 10m, turning westward and head

Comino Island

for the reef wall in front of you. There will be large rocks all around and you will come to various small caverns on your left *(see Site 66)*.

After exploring these head north over the rocks back out to deeper water, finally passing Mushroom Rock. Continue north to the sand, turning north-east back to your waiting boat.

Alternate routes

If pre-arranged you can end the dive by going through the tunnel and into Crystal Lagoon, meeting your boat there — red route. This dive can also be started from the shallower water on the eastern side of the island — the blue route — thus encircling it.

Flying gurnard (Dactylopterus volitans)

Details

Max depth 6–20m *(20–65ft)*
Duration 40–70 min
★ EASY DIVE

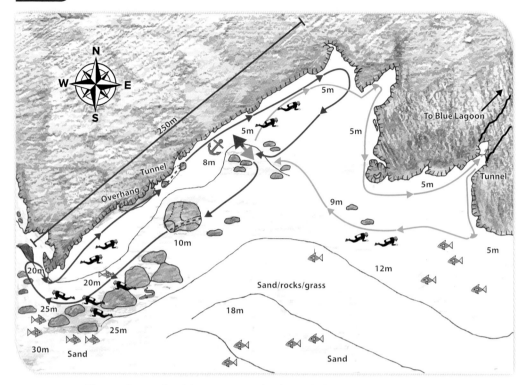

The southern side of Cominotto marks the end of a split-level reef about 250m in length. This area is not often dived but it may be of use in a north-westerly wind, with the cliffs providing a sheltered place to moor.

Dive

The dive starts in shallow water with colourful rock formations and large areas of neptune grass in the sunny, clear blue water. Looking out from the reef wall in a south-easterly direction at 10m there is a large boulder with holes in it — a small swim-through. This leads down to a bank at about 13m and a sloping drop-off made up of sand and small rocks which goes down to about 30m.

The reef wall itself offers great hiding places for moray eel, Mediterranean lobster and octopus. The open water often has schools of barracuda and other predatory fish. Rock formations along the top of the wall have many small cracks, overhangs and holes within the rocks making this yet another playground to be explored.

Turning back with the reef wall on our left shoulder, you will come across an overhang and a small tunnel at a depth of about 5m. Follow the wall back shallow to your waiting boat where you can also do your safety stop.

It may not be possible to do the whole length of this reef in one dive. Depending on qualification and experience you may also include the 60m tunnel at the north-eastern end. It leads to the Blue Lagoon, but you don't want to end up in there — you would need to come back to your waiting boat. It's very shallow the further in you go, and the lagoon is cordoned off to stop boats entering.

Comino Island

North-eastern tunnel which leads to the Blue Lagoon

Striped barracuda (Sphyraena viridensis)

Details
A very pleasant and easy dive.
Max depth 10–40m *(30–130ft)*
Duration 40–60 min
★★ EASY DIVE

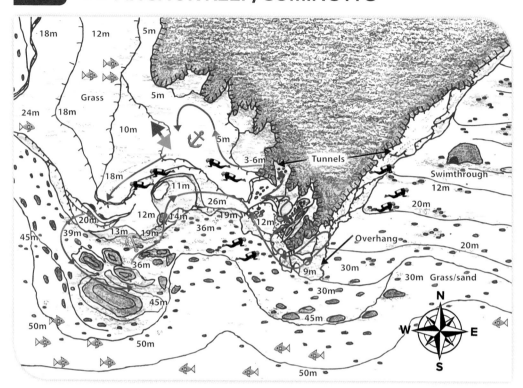

This dive starts on a plateau at 10–12m. Follow the reef south-west over to its edge at 19m. From a dip in the surface here, enter one of two narrow tunnels that exit onto the top of the reef at 20–22m. Then drop down the reef wall to the bottom at 39m.

Turning left/easterly, there are two large rocks at 37m with a swim-through. Just a few metres after this on your right you will find a large old four-pointed anchor. It lies at 36m on a sand and rock bottom, near to the reef wall.

The reef then starts to bank up in steps to 19m. Between 14 and 11m you will see a circular cut-out in the reef. After exploring it, keep following the edge until at 12m you reach another cut-out with several gulleys and overhangs. There will be small rocks dotted about. Turn north-west and head up onto the plateau. In places this is only 5m in depth. Look for the small tunnel at 7m. Then head to your waiting boat.

Comino Island

Painted comber (Serranus scriba)

Diver at play; nudibranch (Chromodoris krohni)

Atlantic lizardfish (Synodus saurus)

Details

Strong currents may occur here. An SMB is essential due to boat traffic.
Max depth 10–50m *(33–165ft)*
Duration 40–60 min
★★ ADVANCED DIVE

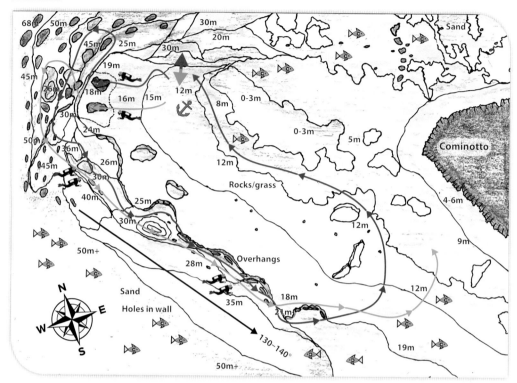

Situated about 250m from the northern most tip of Cominotto, this is a dive I could do time and time again. The entry point is not marked by a buoy and your boat will usually use a depth finder to mark the spot at which they will drop the anchor. The boat may or may not stop there depending on your plan and whether or not there is a current.

Dive

Descend onto the reef and head in a north-westerly direction until you reach the edge. At 17m two large holes on the top of the reef lead down into a spectacular cavern that opens out to large rocks with old fishing nets caught on them. Look out for nudibranchs and slipper lobsters on the cavern roof. The many holes hold an array of fish species.

On exiting the cavern, turn slightly to your right and follow down and around a large rock, the top of which is at a depth of about 26m. From here turn to your left/south-west and the reef undulates in steps to varying depths. Keep the reef wall on your left above you as you gradually shallow up, the rocks tend to peter out and get smaller the further south-west you go.

Swim along at your desired depth and the rocks will dissipate leaving only grass, sand and some fan shells. There are then a series of overhangs and small caverns at intervals for about 100m at depths between 24 and 15m.

You will see the reef on your left get steeper until there is a sheer drop and the reef turns to the right. At this point turn left/north-easterly towards shallower water.

The topography here starts as grass with patches of bare rock, leading to sparse vegetation and life in the shallower depths.

Transparent sea squirt (Clavelina lepadiformis)

One of the holes in the reef; nudibranch (Flabellina pedata)

Details

Currents here can be quite strong from the north-west or south-east so an SMB can be quite useful on this dive.

Max depth 15–50m *(50-165ft)*

Duration 40–60 min

★★ ADVANCED DIVE

Spiny seahorse (Hippocampus guttulatus)

One of the first things a seahorse does when you approach it is to turn its back to you hoping you cannot see it. Approach slowly and carefully not less than a metre away making sure not to disturb it. If you sit quietly it will settle, but **DO NOT surround it**, a semi-circle is better so the seahorse can move away if it wants to. Sadly, many divers are impatient and cause the animal unnecessary stress. If it does move off **DO NOT chase it**, this is disturbance and it is against the law. When the seahorse is stationary, you **MUST NOT hover over it or cause a downdraught** with your fins. Be aware there may be more than one seahorse around you. It is against the law to touch a seahorse or to cause it any harm. **DO NOT shine a torch** on them.

When photographing seahorses **flash guns and strobes are NOT permitted**, as this can also stress them. To actively seek out seahorses and photograph them, a licence is required.

Once you have viewed it move on and around slowly making sure not to disturb it. Stress is shown in seahorses when their colour starts to darken and they bend their head to present less of a profile. Seahorses naturally carry within them diseases like *Vibrio* and Tuberculosis (TB). If a seahorse is stressed, one of these diseases may take hold of the weakened animal with long-term affects, including its eventual death. Under normal conditions these diseases lay dormant in their bodies and seahorses happily live out their lives without ever being affected by them.

Malta has two species of seahorse, the spiny (*Hippocampus guttulatus*) and the short-snouted (*Hippocampus hippocampus*) both are recognised as Data Deficient (DD) under the Convention on International Trade in Endangered Species (CITES). Responsible, sustainable research is vital to further our knowledge and separate fact from fiction and therefore to securing the long term future of these fragile animals.

Divers can play an important role in the conservation of seahorses by reporting sightings to The Seahorse Trust by emailing neil.seahorses@tesco.net (or see www.theseahorsetrust.org). Doing this every time (even if you see the same seahorses again) is really important in helping to build up a better picture of their behaviour, movements and welfare. Thank you for your help and co-operation in their protection.

ROB SMITH

Mauve stinger (Pelagia noctiluca)

The mauve stinger is perhaps the most common in the western and central Mediterranean. As well as having eight stinging cells, from the underside of the bell are four long frilly mouth lobes called oral arms. These also have stinging cells that paralyze and entangle its food, passing it up groves to the mouth parts. For advice on what to do if you get stung *see page 170.*

Jellyfish are among the oldest species on earth, being about 650 million years old. They are composed of about 90-95 % water, with some salts and proteins and are the top predators of planktonic organisms like crustaceans, copepods, fish lava and eggs.

Spot the Jellyfish

The 'Spot the Jellyfish' campaign was launched in 2010 and aims to increase awareness, especially amongst younger generations in Malta. It looks at local diversity through a hands-on experience, using a citizen science approach. Members of the public are encouraged to report sightings of species around the islands. This data is then used to map and educate for the benefit of all. To learn more visit www.ioikids.net or email ioi-moc@gmail.com.

Spot the Alien Fish

Another citizen science project being run by Prof Alain Deidun from the University of Malta is 'Spot the Alien Fish'. Launched in 2016, this campaign addresses non-native fish species which are entering via the Suez Canal and the Strait of Gibraltar. The ultimate aim is to monitor any long-term population changes. Your observations and photographs of alien fish should be sent to aliensmalta@gmail.com.

Nature of Gozo

Posidonia Oceanica

Also known as Neptune grass or Mediterranean tape weed, *Posidonia oceanica* is a seagrass species endemic to the Mediterranean. It forms large underwater meadows that are an important part of the ecosystem: it is protective as it slows down wave movement, prevents erosion and stores carbon. It also traps sediment, 'filtering' it out of the water. It is a good indicator of the state of the environmental as it only grows in unpolluted waters. It doesn't need much light so is found from 1m down to 40m. It is slow growing. Traditionally, *Posidonia oceanica* was harvested for various uses including as a packing material, insulation and medical applications.

Geology of the Maltese Islands

Geologically-speaking the islands are relatively young, with the oldest rock only dating back to the Tertiary period and composed mainly of marine sedimentary rocks. Although the sedimentary platform the islands are situated on was formed during the Triassic period, there are no surface outcrops of this age. All exposed rocks were deposited during the Oligocene and Miocene periods, 30–35 million years ago. The most recent deposits are quaternary, of terrestrial origin and are found in minor quantities. The resultant rock formations are relatively simple and consist of five basic layers laid one-on-top-of-the-other in a layer-cake sequence that have been eroded over many thousands of years. These are:

1. Lower Coralline Limestone—the oldest exposed rock, outcropping to a height of 140m in the vertical cliffs near Xlendi and Sannat.
2. Globigerina Limestone—the second oldest rock covering approximately 70 % of the island, eroding to give a broad, gently rolling landscape. Variations in the thickness of this formation are considerable, ranging from 23m near Fort Chambray to 207m around Marsaxlokk in Malta. This rock consists of yellow to pale-grey limestone comprising of planktonic *globigerinid foraminifera*. The formation is divided into lower, middle and upper globigerina limestone by two beds of phosphorite pebbles.
3. Blue Clay—overlies the globigerina limestone formation. It erodes easily when wet and forms a sloping mass of rock fragments at the foot of a cliff that flow out over the underlying rock. Variations in thickness are considerable ranging from 75m at Xaghra, to nil in eastern Malta, where upper coralline limestone rests directly on globigerina limestone. Deposition of blue clay may have occurred in an open muddy water environment with water depths up to 150m for the lower part of the formation.
4. Greensand—consists of biolistic limestone rich in glauconite deposited in a warm sea. Un-weathered sections are green but get oxidised to an orange colour when exposed.
5. Upper Coralline Limestone—the youngest Tertiary formation in the islands reaching the thickness of approximately 160m. The strata are very similar to the lowest stratum in the Maltese Islands. It is also renowned for the abundance of the fossil algae species found. It resembles the lower coralline limestone both on chemical and paleontological grounds, indicating deposition in shallow waters. The transition from the underlying greensands is gradual, sometimes merging into red and black granular sandstone; or red and white coralline rich limestone, which passes into a white calcareous sandstone—compact, soft or porous but always rich in organic remains.

Though some layers are completely crystalline and have lost traces of the organisms from which they originated, other portions contain casts of shells and other organisms, such as sand dollars found at Dwejra.

The geology of Gozo is more varied than that of Malta, with more frequent outcrops of blue clay being a characteristic feature.

Ambulance/Fire/Police — 112
Gozo Police, Republic Street, Victoria — +356 21 562040
Hospital (Gozo General) — +356 21 561700
Hyperbaric Chamber — +356 21 561600 (Gozo) or +356 25 455205 (Malta)
Armed Forces Malta (AFM) — +356 21 824220/1

Unaccompanied diving considerations

1. **Qualification** — must be PADI AOW, CMAS 2 Star Diver or another organisation's equivalent.
2. **Oxygen** units and **first aid** — can be hired from most centres. SMBs or DSMBs are required.
3. **Spare equipment** — carry spares e.g. fin and mask straps etc., and a small tool set.

Medical emergencies

1. Assess the situation/form a plan;
1. Act on your plan;
2. Delegate areas of responsibility;
3. Provide basic life support and attend to injuries;
4. Control the scene;
5. Evacuate the patient by the most appropriate method. N.B. it may be quicker to take a patient to Accident and Emergency in cases of suspected DCI, although the chamber is required for re-compression.

Suspected decompression illness (DCI)

Primary variables — forced/rapid ascent, depth, bottom time, buddy's input, make assessment. **Secondary factors** — fatigue, dehydration, vigorous exercise, cold, age, illness, injuries, alcohol, obesity.

First aid for suspected DCI

Conscious — Lay them down, administer 100 % oxygen, monitor and manage shock, contact emergency medical service (EMS) on 112. **Unresponsive but breathing** — left side down and support head, use continuous flow oxygen at 15 litres per minute. Monitor and contact EMS on 112. **Not breathing** — administer two rescue breaths and 30 chest compressions at a rate of 100 per minute. Contact EMS on 112.

For suspected emergencies call for an ambulance or take the victim immediately to the Accident & Emergency Dept., Gozo General Hospital in Victoria. Staff will make an assessment. The EU funded the Hyperbaric Unit at the hospital to promote safety within the diving industry. It is operated by fully trained staff and open 24 hours a day, 7 days a week.

First aid for jellyfish stings

1. Carefully wash but **do not rub** the sting site with seawater. You may see bullae (blisters in lines or streaks); **2.** Remove any stinging cells by scraping the skin with a plastic/credit card or using sticky tape; **3.** If available apply a baking soda slurry (form a paste from 50 % soda 50 % seawater). This may prevent further envenomation from any stinging tentacles still attached; **4.** Consider immersion in cold seawater; **5.** Apply ice packs wrapped in a cloth or tea towel.

Index

Spiny lobster (Palinurus elephas)

Mediterranean/fried egg jellyfish (Cotylorhiza tuberculata)

OCEANFOTO.CO.UK

Walking sea hare (Aplysia juliana)

Atlantic stargazer (Uranoscopus scaber)

Snakelocks anemone (Anemonia viridis)

Long-spine slate pen sea urchin (Cidaris cidaris)

Index

Mediterranean hermit crab
(Dardanus arrosor)

DENNIS WILTSHIRE

Nudibranch (Felimare picta)

Atlantic bluefin tuna (Thunnus thynnus)

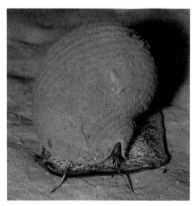

Tun snail (Tonna galea)

Red scorpionfish (Scorpaena scrofa)

Wide-eyed flounder (Bothus podas)

Common octopus amongst cnidarians, sponges and algaes

Anemone goby (Gobius bucchichi)

Brown sea star (Astropecten spinulosus)

Mediterranean red sea star (Echinaster sepositus)

Golden Balearic/bandtooth conger (Ariosoma balearicum)

Damselfish (Chromis chromis)